Daniel Jay Baum

WAREHOUSES FOR DEATH
The Nursing Home Industry

Burns & MacEachern Ltd.

Canadian Cataloguing in Publication Data

Baum, Daniel Jay, 1934-
    Warehouses for death

Includes index.
Bibliography: p.
ISBN 0-88768-072-0

1. Nursing homes — Canada.   2. Old age homes —
Canada.   3. Aged — Canada.   I. Title.

RA998.C2B38   362.6'15'0971   C77-000159-9

CONTENTS

INTRODUCTION   IX
CHAPTER 1 ✓   Welcome to Our "Home"   1
CHAPTER 2 ✓   Homes Taken — Homes
                   Given   13
CHAPTER 3 ✓   Point of no Return:
                   Entering a Home   27
CHAPTER 4 ✓   Life in the "Home":
                   Confinement   40
CHAPTER 5 ✓   Law: Words Alone?   57
CHAPTER 6 ⌐   A Matter of Dollars:
                   Shaping Public Policy   72

A PORTFOLIO OF PHOTOGRAPHS
BY ANDREW DANSON   88

CHAPTER 7   The Physician and the
                   Coroner   98
CHAPTER 8   New Beginnings   108
EPILOGUE

NOTES   Chapter One   122
             Chapter Two   129
             Chapter Three   135
             Chapter Four   145
             Chapter Five   149
             Chapter Six   160
             Chapter Seven   168
             Chapter Eight   178

BIBLIOGRAPHY   182
INDEX   186

INTRODUCTION

WAREHOUSES FOR DEATH is an abrasive title; it shocks. If only this were not necessary. How much better it would be to write of a caring society where the old are accepted and loved. But, relative to its population, Canada holds a commanding position among other comparable countries for institutionalizing its aged citizens.

It is no act of love to put the old in institutions. It is no remarkable achievement that the old are no longer left to languish in cold water flats as they await death. Nor is there any necessary correlation between the dollars spent on health care and the good health of the aged. The aged in institutions may survive in body, but this does not mean that they survive in mind and spirit.

It is not the purpose of this book to write only of problems nor to exploit the horror stories concerning the institutionalized aged, but to describe institutions, such as nursing homes, and to ask if there is not a better way to treat the elderly.

In writing the book many gave their help. I wish to thank all of them and to name a few. In doing so, however, I alone bear responsibility for the pages that follow. Ms. Linda Grobovsky for several years served as a social worker in Toronto. Her job regularly brought her into contact with the aged. During the school year 1976-1977 Ms. Grobovsky was enrolled in the certificate programme of Osgoode Hall Law School. As part of that programme she acted as a research assistant for the study that resulted in this book. Her experience and realistic critique were invaluable.

Other research assistants who contributed to the legal and historical analysis are Stephen Nesbitt, David Simpson, Gene Coleman, Bill Doyle, Howard Isaac, Nancy Backhouse and Don Malamet, THANKS.

Finally, I wish to thank Ms. Sheryl Shulman who typed several drafts of this manuscript under difficult conditions.

DANIEL J. BAUM

Toronto
August 29, 1977

CHAPTER ONE

Welcome to Our "Home"

*"Canada could earn the questionable distinction of having more
of its elderly citizens in institutions . . . than almost any other
industrialized country in the world. Is this really necessary?"*
Nathan Markus, 1974.

Another Way: Respect for Self[1]

With his internationally known visitor, a British specialist in geriatrics,
the minister of welfare walked through the model nursing home. They
saw a man in his fifties in a wheel chair. He was alone, staring straight
ahead. He had been in the nursing home for *fifteen years*, shut up with
the older people because his case, like theirs, was considered hopeless.
He had multiple sclerosis, and earlier medical examination had
indicated that he would never be able to walk again. Because he had lost
his productive capacity he was a charge on society, so the least
expensive place to keep him was at a nursing home.

The doctor from Britain, however, noticed only a slight tremor. Was
it so certain that the man could never walk again?

> I asked him to straighten his knees and bend them. He was able to
> do this . . . I asked him whether he could walk. He replied
> emphatically that he could not. He informed us that he had not
> walked for fifteen years. Yet, he could straighten and bend both
> his knees without much difficulty, and fully bend his ankle joints
> up and down.
>
> So we suggested, very gently, that he try utilizing the services
> of myself and the then Minister of Welfare as a physical aid . . .
> We got him to stand. The Minister was a little surprised. The
> Minister had it clearly in his own mind that after fifteen years, this
> was one of the chronic sick. Still, with our assistance, the patient
> was able to stand.
>
> And then we assisted him to a table and suggested that he take
> three side-ways steps to the right with our psychological support
> rather than our physical support. This he did. Then he took three
> steps to the left, and sat down. A little later we suggested that,
> with assistance, he walk across the room. Now, by this time the
> patient was very surprised as was the Minister, who turned to me

and said: "What is this man doing in this situation?" I tactfully had no answer.

There was an answer. A patient's condition can change and a medical diagnosis may not forever remain accurate. At the very least, regular observation is necessary. More to the point, however, is the fact that medical examination can be terribly incomplete if it attempts only to probe the body with a view toward labelling and uniform treatment. It is necessary to understand the patient's capacity for rehabilitation; to know the whole human being; and to direct medical effort toward restoring the person to his or her community.

Prognoses can become self-fulfilling. Before 1944, for example, the common view was that paraplegia and quadraplegia resulted in death in about eighteen months. The patient was bedridden and neglected, slowly sedated to death, deprived of the will to live.

Change the treatment, and the result often can be different. Put the emphasis on rehabilitation as far as possible, on return to the community, and the medical diagnosis will also change. A will to live can be nurtured. The sick can see themselves as alive.

This does not mean that the patient will always recover. But there is no reason why he or she cannot live those remaining days a competent functioning person within a known and warm community.

Mrs. Franck was a *young* lady of 72 who was sent by her physician to a chronic care hospital to die. But Mrs. Franck wanted to live. She knew that the cancer which had already resulted in a massive mastectomy would kill her within a year. Still, in the time remaining Mrs. Franck wanted to care for herself.

At the hospital she did not want nurses. She insisted on attending to her own needs, fixing her own bed, walking to the dining room for meals, and mixing with other patients. Yet what Mrs. Franck wanted most was to return to her own bungalow where she lived alone. She told the doctor this, and he, not without some apprehension, released her from the hospital, asking her to report there once a week; he also informed her general physician.

Mrs. Franck went home where she was content. There she stayed for about four months. The cancer caused a respiratory infection and a bit more stridor. She returned to the hospital for care. Again, however, she attended to her own needs as far as possible.

All at the hospital knew that she was dying. Their concern, though, was to sustain a life as long as possible. A few months later, somewhat more frail but still coping, Mrs. Franck tugged at the hospital doctor's sleeve: "I want to go home again."

The doctor was put on the spot. The hospital staff were getting anxious and guilty.

Dared I do this? [the doctor asked]. Was it appropriate? Well, the staff and I had a discussion and we determined to follow the patient's judgment. We had none of our own. Off she went. She stayed at home another three months. She came back again with more stridor. . . . She wanted to go to her single room again. She was measuring her physical competence and her motivation far more accurately than I was. Though a doctor, I was in error; I was in doubt. I was anxious. I was guilt-laden. I said the same, somewhat anxiously: "All right, go to your room; make your own bed; keep your room tidy." This Mrs. Franck did meticulously. Now I weakened. I had promised Mrs. Franck no nursing attention, but I always had an occupational therapist going in and out of her unit every three or four hours to see what was going on. But on Mrs. Franck went, her complexion was a deep olive green with cyanosis. One day as I was doing a clinical round I was asked to go over to her unit immediately. She had collapsed, after having made her bed. She was in a coma due to liver failure. We moved her to the intensive care unit . . . where she died four and a half days after last making her bed . . . a very happy woman.

The doctor could have managed differently. He could have placed her in a bed and let her stare at the ceiling. But this, in the doctor's words, is fatal. "It kills more people than anything else at all."

The Canadian Way: More Institutions[2]

With few exceptions, however, Canadians have placed increasing numbers in nursing homes, homes for the aged and charitable institutions caring for the elderly. People are there to die. Once they walk through the nursing home door and take their rooms, they will not walk out again. They are stripped of their assets, given a small personal allowance, promised minimal nursing care, regulated severely in their routine and medicated to institutional compliance. In a very real sense, they are encapsulated and warehoused for death. They are removed from the community, and the community accordingly does not have to see either old age or death.

According to the United Nations, a country is considered old if more than 8 per cent of its population is over 65. By this definition Canada entered the club of old nations with the 1971 census. By the year 2001, if present low birth rates continue, almost 12 per cent of the Canadian population will be over 65. And by 2031 that percentage will have increased to 20 per cent of the population. Translated into numbers, the percentages become even more alarming. By the year 2001, Canada's elderly population will have doubled from the 1971 level of 1.7 million to about 3.3 million. Of those over 85 years old and thus more likely to need intensive care, the projected increase is from 142,000 in 1971 to 351,000 in 2001.

This places an enormous financial drain on society, and in time that drain may become one which society, that is, those who make up the power base, the taxpayers, will no longer tolerate. The Long Range Health Planning Branch of the Ministry of Health and Welfare estimated in 1974 that if present trends continue, in 1986 those over 65 will make up 9.8 per cent of Canada's population. This over-65 group will take 38.6 per cent of the patient days[3] in general and allied special hospitals. By 2001, the corresponding percentages will have increased to 10.9 per cent and 42.0 per cent respectively. In other words, in proportion to their numbers in the population, those over 65 will be using four times their number of hospital beds.

Excluded from Life[4]

At 65, a person is condemned to be "old" by our society. But does it follow that the 65-year-old in fact loses capacity at that age, and is unable to function? There are examples enough of full lives in later years. Only recently "Ma" Murray, of Lillooet, British Columbia, came out of retirement to found and edit a newspaper — at the age of 91. And of course the former prime minister of Canada, now a staunch spokesman for the opposition, John Diefenbaker, has never retired — in his eighties.

If the senior citizen is given a chance to remain in the economic and social mainstream, age probably will come slowly. (There is every reason to believe that almost until the point of death the old will be able to function independently and well. This certainly is what the "old" desire.) In 1972, fourteen years into its longitudinal study, the Ontario Long Term Study of Aging asked 1,300 of the original 2,500 subjects, many of whom were then about 53 years old and reflected a variety of backgrounds, about the life style they desired in later years. "Four-fifths emphasized that (older people want to live apart from their families to enjoy their independence and to avoid conflict in life styles) . . . For three-fifths of the study group, the ideal living quarters for seniors is their own home. . . . A small proportion suggested retirement communities."

But at age 65, for nearly all, there will be no choice. Rather, there will be forced retirement from the labour force — for those lucky enough to have remained employed. (In time the retirement age probably will be lowered as jobs become even more scarce. In 1976 the unemployment rate in Canada climbed to a recession high of about 8 per cent.)

Perhaps 30 to 40 per cent of the "defined" labour force will receive a pension following retirement. For most women who have chosen the role of housewife as a career there will be only the security that comes to the husband. In 1975 the poverty line in Canada was $2,520 for an individual and $4,199 for a couple. In that year, more than half the Canadians over 65 needed federal assistance *to bring them to the poverty line*. And it must be stressed that this in itself is an artificial line. It does not allow people a decent standard of living but is drawn to create a rough form of justice for those unable to fend for themselves.

The plight of the newly retired "senior citizen" is grim. The husband stands excluded from the work force facing poverty with a wife still dependent on him. The 65-year-old couple must feel enormous tension and fear.

The man, in particular, is disorientated. Employed one day as a productive worker holding seniority and responsibility, he finds himself the next day, solely because of age, forced into unemployment. What is the retired person to do? It will take more than initiative and imagination to break down the barriers that society has created as a means for distributing scarce jobs.

Not only does the husband experience the emotional jolt that comes from not having a job; he faces the very real danger that money will not be available simply to hold what he has taken years to acquire. In studies conducted by the Canadian Senate Special Committee on Aging in 1961, it was found that about half of those families whose head was aged 65 were living in their own homes. Even where the older person was single or alone as a result of widowhood or children leaving home, nearly 43 per cent continued to maintain their own dwelling. Of those who did own their own homes, however, the majority had finished paying for them.

In spite of this, the inflation level at the time of the Senate study was nearly as sharp as that of 1976, and the economic crunch felt by the older home owner was severe. The Central Mortgage Housing Corporation found too that a substantial percentage of homes owned by those over 65 were "much below average." Nearly 7 per cent were in need of repair. Well over 25 per cent were without a separate toilet.

Close to 30 per cent lacked a separate bath or shower. The Senate Committee estimated that about 300,000 houses occupied by elderly families were in an unsatisfactory condition and needed repair.

(In this connection, the president of the Central Housing Mortgage Corporation made an interesting comment to the Senate Committee: ". . . it must be remembered that North America is still not far removed from the pioneer community where the quality of a man's home was regarded to be the results of his own endeavours. This is still fairly well ingrained . . . this is one of the things that retards the growth of public insistence of adequate housing for the poor.'')

Rather than see their homes continue to deteriorate, the elderly, most of whom (70 per cent) live in urban areas, may feel compelled to sell — only to find that their lot is not easier but more difficult. They will search for cheap quarters; they likely will take small flats or one-room apartments in deteriorating neighbourhoods. And even there, aside from the shock of leaving familiar surroundings for those that are unknown and where neighbours may even be hostile, there is a gnawing fear that the rent may be increased or, worst still, the building torn down to make way for redevelopment.

For certainly half of all Canadians over 65 the harsh reality is rejection by the community. They live alone; they they live in fear; they live in poverty. Their younger neighbours may see squalid quarters and "for the sake" of the elderly residents urge their removal to a "nice clean home for the aged." A Toronto social worker told this story:

I will never forget my anguish over the way one elderly couple survived. Their flat was bug infested. Medications were in frightening abundance, and they were probably improperly used. Social and nutritional needs were neglected. I attempted to provide service after service. I tried to convince them to enter a nursing home so that they could be properly cared for. I also had to deal with other people in the community who wanted to know why I was not putting the elderly couple somewhere.

The elderly couple rejected all of the services that I offered. They rejected as well my idea of their entering a nursing home. Three years from the time I first saw them I must say that their outward condition is precisely the same. Their vision and physical health seem the same. The couple's neighbours still call my office questioning why the couple cannot be placed somewhere safe.

Their flat is filthy, and by my standards they are terribly isolated. But they are still alive and at this point in time I am sure that this is due to the fact that they are still exercising choice as to how and where to live. Had they been deprived of choice (and they might have been), I might have caused them a great deal of harm.

Basic Needs: At-Home Care[5]

The needs of the elderly, like those of us all, are basic. But their struggle for survival is intensified in a society that has gone rather far in forcing their isolation, dependence and poverty. Yet, for all the isolation, there are many among the over-65s who prefer to remain in their own homes, however squalid.

The internationally known doctor who toured some of Canada's nursing homes with a provincial minister operates his day hospital in Britain to allow the old to stay in their homes. He spoke of Mr. Saul, aged 93. He lives alone in a dilapidated cottage. When Mr. Saul's wife died his niece of 73 came to live with him. But in time she became confused and was placed in a nursing home where she died after about eight months. The geriatric liaison health officer was very interested in Mr. Saul:

It is appreciated that he is greatly at risk due to age and increasing infirmity in a very inadequate environment. But he does not feel a need to change his lifestyle. His housing is an isolated stone house on the edge of the village. He pays a "peppercorn" rent annually. [The custom of paying a token annual rent of a peppercorn or a rose originated in the Middle Ages.] There is no electricity. Lighting is by gas in the living room only. Heating comes from a coal fire in the living room. There is a well and a privy in the garden. They are sited at some distance from each other. You really can't think of a more terrible situation.

Mr. Saul has poor vision. Yet each night, to go to bed, he must negotiate a difficult staircase with the aid of a flashlight. A nephew and his wife live about a mile from Mr. Saul. *They are employed by the Home Health Service* to give domestic help and supervision. One visits each morning, and the other comes in the evening to fetch coal and water. On Sundays they cook a meal for him. His nearest neighbour does the necessary shopping and keeps a discreet eye on him — without invading his privacy. The local health visitor comes weekly; the district health nurse often drops by on weekends; and his general practitioner visits monthly.

Three times a week Mr. Saul is taken to the day hospital which he particularly enjoys in the winter. (In the summer he potters in his garden.) The British doctor drew these conclusions: Mr. Saul is a very independent man. He wants to remain in his home, but this is becoming increasingly difficult. Still, local health authorities are doing their best to accommodate Mr. Saul, and have increased their vigilance. The doctor offered Mr. Saul the opportunity to come to the day hospital five times a week. Mr. Saul refused. He prefers to be at home. "He didn't see why he should be interfered with at all by all these therapeutic services! This is Mr. Saul with his hearing aid."

Britain's approach is not Canada's. Nathan Markus wrote in 1974: "If present trends continue, and unless new policies on domiciliary and community services for old people are developed and implemented, Canada could earn the questionable distinction of having more of its elderly citizens in institutions (special care facilities, nursing homes and mainly, homes for the aged) than almost any other industrialized country in the world. . . . Is this really necessary?"

Canada must decide the extent to which older people should be helped to remain in the open community. (In 1976 a firm of management consultants estimated that one in ten Ontario patients could be removed from hospitals — if there were adequate outpatient service.) In many countries in continental Europe, as well as the United Kingdom, the trend is toward intensifying and expanding community services aimed at maintaining older people in their homes. There, the popular belief is that home life is philosophically, psychologically and socially preferable to institutional life. At his own day care hospital the British doctor just mentioned was able to cut the number of days spent in his hospital from about 300 days per patient to 35 and, in the process, increase the number of outpatients, while cutting the average cost of treatment for each patient by about half.

Writing in the *Canadian Journal of Public Health*, C. W. Schwenger stated:

> 1971 statistics from Great Britain indicate that of those over 65 living at home no less than 7.4 per cent were attended by Health Visitors (Public Health Nurses in Canada), 9.1 per cent by Home Nurses (Victorian Order of Nurses) and 13.9 per cent by Chiropodists. I defy anyone to compare these statistics with what we have available in Canada and not blush . . . It is disturbing to compare 7.4 per cent of the elderly (over 65) attended at home by health visitors in Great Britain in 1971 with an estimate of *1 per cent* visited by Public Health Nurses in Ontario in 1965. A recent study in two rural counties in Ontario still showed less than 2 per cent of the elderly were visited by Public Health Nurses from the local health department in 1973. This in spite of the fact that those

over 65 comprised 13 to 14 per cent of the total population of these counties and had much greater than average health needs.

What is to be done with the old? A senior nurse consultant for the province of Ontario wrote in a confidential memorandum dated June 1976:

Many elderly disabled and infirm residents of this Province could be successfully maintained in their own homes rather than in institutions, if certain ⸤health and supportive services were available.⸥ It should be recognized that the availability of monies through the Extended Care Plan [see Chapter 3] has led to a general increase in the demand for long term beds in Ontario, and people being forced to go into institutions because of this insurance scheme. *That is, we pay people to put their aged relatives into nursing homes and homes for the aged, while on the other hand charge them to get home nursing, home care services or attend Day Hospitals and Centres where they exist.*

The effort put into support services designed to keep the old in their homes is fragmented, underfinanced, and underutilized. In 1975 it was estimated that only 0.2 to 0.5 per cent of those over 65 in Canada made use of the welter of home care services. How can it be otherwise? Aside from specialized family service organizations with their unique understanding of the welfare bureaucracy, who knows where to turn? The research coordinator for the Federal-Provincial Working Group on Home Care Programs said that in Canada no centralized body administers these programmes. Rather, they are administered by regional and provincial public health personnel, by hospitals, by voluntary agencies, by independent community boards and by district medical societies. The necessary finance comes largely from provincial governments, and the remaining funds are derived from private charitable agencies such as the Salvation Army.

Even more to the point, however, are the mix of goals of home care programmes. (And there should be no mistake that the goal determines the nature of the service.) For example, if the goal is to reduce hospital use, homemaking and visiting nurse services will be provided but only so long as is necessary to care for the *medical* problem of the patient — as defined by the doctor. The care will end when the medical problem is brought to an end. The more difficult problem of a stroke victim being integrated into family and neighbourhood life may remain, and, in time, be subject to that final treatment — admission to a nursing home.

The Canadian Senate Special Committee on Aging estimated that in

1962-63 about 7.7 per cent of Canadians over 65 were living in some form of institution. Some provinces were well above this average. The figure for Ontario was 8.5 per cent; for Alberta, 9.3 per cent. A decade later the percentages had not diminished. (In Great Britain, the 1961 rate was 4.5 per cent, less than half that of Ontario.)

There can be little doubt that the emphasis in Ontario and Alberta, two of Canada's wealthiest provinces, is on the institutionalization of the old. This is not to say that provincial governments have clamped down on funds for home services. Quite the contrary. Budgets for such services have been increased. The important point, again, is one of emphasis. Public policy is directed not toward integration of those over 65 but rather toward their isolation and exclusion.

Why is this so? Why are basic civil rights defined to exclude the elderly? Indeed, many provinces have no civil rights laws affecting age discrimination. Those which have such laws allow discrimination after the age of 65. Is the basis solely one of economics, that is, because there are relatively few jobs, the old should be expected to give way to the young?

Does job scarcity explain the totality of exclusion? Does job scarcity explain the willingness of the community to opt for *higher institutional cost* compared to the lower cost for maintaining a person at home? In Ontario about $21 per day is paid to maintain the overwhelming number of residents in nursing homes and homes for the aged. Of this, the government health subsidy is $13.60 (in 1976). The $21 represents only the cost of maintenance. It does not include the cost of constructing buildings, of capital plant. In many provinces the government owns and operates either a large number or all of the nursing home facilities.

In 1971, Ontario, for example, had more than 46,000 beds, in nursing homes and homes for the aged, for those over 65. It has been estimated that by 1985 another 27,000 beds will be needed. The cost to the province and the individual will be enormous. All of the nursing homes and homes for the aged receiving the government health subsidy do so on the basis that their residents are in need of the statutory minimum care. Why cannot such care be given in the resident's own home? Think of what $13.60 a day would buy for a person over 65.

Capital expenditures also would be drastically reduced. If 27,000 more beds are projected for the year 1986, this means that about two hundred new nursing homes or homes for the aged will have to be constructed. Why are the old institutionalized and hospitalized? Why does society feel humane about its purposeful isolation of the aged?

Laws have long existed which require children on coming of age to care for incapacitated parents. More recently in Ontario the government has proposed tougher enforcement of those laws. In point of fact it should also be said that a very large number of older people do live with their children. Yet, having said this, there is no denying the willingness both of the government and the citizenry — within a cost range — to increase the number of institutions for the aged.

Indeed, it is rather remarkable to observe the willingness of Canadian breadwinners to assume such obligations. This society faces a decreasing number of people (that is, productive workers) bearing responsibility for an increasing number of individuals, namely, the young and the old, and those women who have opted for the role of housewife without pay. The 1971 census not only forecast an increasingly large older population but showed that those between the ages of 0 to 24 comprise about 17.43 per cent of the population. These groups are dependent on the rest of the community for their support because jobs have been denied them. In conservative terms, about 25 per cent of the Canadian population is dependent on the remaining 75 per cent.

And it must be stressed that these figures are conservative for the following reasons: first, the employment of most women (60 per cent) is marriage. Of those women in the labour force, it is fairly clear that most are part-time employees. This is suggested by their earnings. According to the 1970 Canadian Senate Report on Poverty, 48 per cent of the women who were engaged in year-round employment earned less than $3,000. Secondly, in Canada one in every four persons is poor. This includes children under the age of 16 (36 per cent of the poor), and two-thirds of those over 65 who fell beneath the 1967 poverty line. Thirdly, in 1976 the unemployment rate rose to about 8 per cent — at least half of whom were characterized as young-unemployed.

There are no precise means for measuring the dependence of the old (and the young) on the remaining portion of the population. But while the 25 per cent figure can be accepted as a conservative estimate, it is not unrealistic to estimate that the percentage could be as high as 40 to 45 per cent. Working Canadians already support non-working Canadians — wives, children and parents — in their private capacity. They support non-working Canadians publicly, through the state, by means of taxes which provide the revenues for social benefits such as homes for the aged, old age pensions and general welfare.

The working Canadian finds himself pressured enormously. He is already precluded from entering the work force on a full-time, well-paid basis until he reaches the age of about 25. Then he must make himself highly mobile. By the end of the century he will have to move perhaps as frequently as once every three years simply to maintain a job in an ever changing industrial world.

In addition, the demands of industry will make the worker prone to early obsolescence. And industry and unions alike will desire retirement at earlier and earlier ages. (Some unions already are pressing for retirement at age 55.) Yet at this age the breadwinner will very likely have dependent children as well as a dependent spouse. How can he be expected to care for his dependent parents? And, just as worrying, how can the working Canadian provide for himself — forced to an early retirement, and thanks to modern medicine promised a longer life, a life that might last another twenty to twenty-five years? This is not to say that Canada does not supply a marginal level of income for those unable to provide for themselves. Nor can one deny the reality of a great number of those over 65 who were able to save and plan for a comfortable retirement. But the hard fact is that a large segment of the elderly face poverty and loneliness as they are removed from the economic mainstream.

It is not difficult to understand the pressures which operate to place the old in institutions. In addition to his other troubles, it is difficult for the worker, forced to be mobile, to acquire roots and to become a part of a community. He lives in cities where the cost of living is high. He may incur large long-term debts. He works hard to be able to make a down payment on a home and assume a floating, high-interest, long-term mortgage. Yet he knows that the chances are that his job may not be permanent, and that inflation may shrivel the dollars that he does earn.

The fate of the old, the parents of working Canadians, is also hard. They have not asked to be excluded from the community mainstream. They have not asked to be removed from their children. Yet, in stripping them of the opportunity to earn a living, even to work part-time, society has also stripped them of status. In this country money is not only a means for survival but a status symbol.

With little money and no work, what can the old do except await death? And this is a process that neither their children nor the community want to watch. But in the face of rejection, there is one outstanding fact: the old still choose life — given the chance.

CHAPTER TWO

Homes Taken — Homes Given

"It is important at our stage in life that one have a place to go for a quiet cry in privacy."
A resident of a home for the aged.

Goals and Results[1]

For more than thirty years Mrs. Schramm had been a medical secretary, a job in which she took pride. The hospital for which she worked valued her. It was with sadness that her employer learned of the bone disease that forced Mrs. Schramm to end full-time employment at the age of 64.

"I did not want to leave my job. I loved my work. It made me feel useful, worthwhile. But what was I to do? I couldn't work a full day. I tired too easily. To make matters worse, my pension brought me only $245 a month."

Mrs. Schramm could have sought admission to one of Toronto's homes for the aged. "I didn't want to do this. I didn't feel old then. I don't feel old now. I have a bone disease. I can't sleep much at night. I tire easily. Still, I want to live and not vegetate."

The provincial public housing authority heard of Mrs. Schramm and tried to help. It had housing throughout the city, including senior citizen housing. The case worker thought she had resolved Mrs. Schramm's problem. A senior citizen's one-bedroom apartment was found at the northern edge of the city. The apartment was new, and Mrs. Schramm could move in her own furniture. What is more, Mrs. Schramm would have the pleasure of contact with her peers. Finally, the senior citizens complex offered a wide assortment of activities: daily concerts of classical music; frequent bus trips throughout the city.

The rent that Mrs. Schramm would be required to pay was adjusted so that she would not have to spend all of her pension. There would be enough left for food and some pleasures.

Mrs. Schramm should have been happy but she was not. "I do not have any family as such. I have three friends and they live miles from the apartment. I cannot stay in touch with them . . . I have made the most of the apartment. I have decorated every inch . . . But I don't want to spend my time simply listening to classical music and taking bus trips. . . . For me there is more to life. The hospital will take me back on a part-time basis. I would like very much to do this. But I can't do it living where I am, and the housing authority will not authorize a move elsewhere. I have been told that I should be happy where I am.''

There was an answer for Mrs. Schramm, although not a solution made possible by government. Mrs. Schramm had lived and worked in an area of the city now largely populated by older people. This is not unusual. Many neighbourhoods are stable; the families that originally moved into the area tend to stay. The homes are old, but the mortgages have been paid. Why couldn't Mrs. Schramm move into one of the old and large homes? Wouldn't her company be welcomed either by a couple or a widow her own age?

Mrs. Schramm agreed to explore the possibilities. She had enough income for some rent. For the older and lonely home owner that money, coupled with Mrs. Schramm's company, could be most welcome. The money might be used to brighten and repair the house, and any excess for pleasure. Mrs. Schramm would have removed herself as a charge on the province, and the subsidized apartment on the edge of the city could be rented to another in greater need. Moreover, Mrs. Schramm would have moved to control her own life; she would have maintained her vitality and, in doing so, revitalized the person into whose home she would move.

A minister in the area where Mrs. Schramm wanted to move said that more than half of his congregation were over 70 years old, and of these most were women who owned their homes and were living alone. "Their biggest fear is what will happen if they should become sick. Recently one of these women had a stroke. Her house was simply locked up during the period of her illness. We did our best to handle matters, but I am sure that the job was not adequate.''

The minister's answer to the problem was to try to establish senior citizen housing administered by the church. He had been working on the project for several years, and he had suffered frustration. Politicians would not release funds, and the bureaucracy snarled dedicated planners in a mass of red tape. Still, the minister did not give up. He would make the project a reality; it was a matter of tenacity and faith.

Yet, he asked, why did older people have to be dislocated? Why was it necessary to move them from a home which not only held memories but had taken years of work to obtain? In addition, to own a house is still a badge of dignity; it still represents the capacity of the individual to control his or her own life. Why not make the most of that capacity?

"Take a look at the homes," said the minister. "They were once well cared for. Now they look tattered from the outside. They are in need of paint and the older person simply cannot afford a paint job. The interiors may be in need of plumbing or electrical repairs, but they cannot be made. Can there be any doubt that a senior citizens home, maintained by the church, makes more sense than the anxiety of home ownership?"

Yet a federal-provincial-municipal programme exists to restore neighbourhoods. That programme provides actual grants amounting to as much as $3,500 to home owners to make the very kind of repairs described as necessary by the minister.

The minister smiled sadly, shrugged, and said, "Yes. There is such a programme. But see how it works. It is a pilot programme; it is not fixed. It will end soon. The programme applies only to those municipalities that have opted into it because the cities must pay a small percentage of the overall cost. In Toronto, for example, the city of Toronto has opted into the programme, but the large borough of North York, for reasons that I cannot understand, has elected to stay out of it.

"Now, for a minute consider just how the programme works. The applicant must have a home which is listed as being in a neighbourhood in need of rehabilitation. Next, he or she must complete detailed financial statements and present these statements along with the title to the home. Finally, bids must be obtained from contractors . . . How easy do you think it is for an older person to make application? Against all of this, there is another consideration. People do not like welfare, and this kind of grant is considered welfare."

The minister understood the law and the bureaucracy; less than 1 per cent of eligible over-65 home owners in Toronto applied for home repair grants. Earlier the Senate Report on Aging had made clear the need for such programmes. About half of those over 65 owned their own homes, of which a substantial number were in need of fundamental repair.

Indeed, in the city of Toronto the Mayor's Task Force on the Disabled and Elderly, reporting in 1974, spoke of more than the need simply to refurbish. The committee referred specifically to the need to make housing suitable for the old:

> In housing, as in just about every other area, the handicapped and elderly are victims of ignorance — unintentional, but widespread and profound. People who design and build accommodations — houses, apartments, condominia, townhouses, etc. — do so with the adult healthy person or family in mind; able-bodied people have no problem climbing steps, negotiating twenty-four-inch

doorways, summoning elevators, navigating kitchens and bathrooms, stepping over raised doorsills and making 180-degree turns in confined spaces.

There is no valid reason why most housing could not be designed to accommodate the elderly who are slow in responses. . . .

There is, however, a curious difference between desired goals and public policy. And there is a difference between public policy and its implementation. The Mayor's Task Force could understand and speak of the need for housing designed for the elderly — at comparatively low cost. Yet the programme adopted by the city did relatively little to help those most in need.

Flexible Housing[2]

On a national basis the most important financier of housing is the Central Mortgage and Housing Corporation, a Crown corporation established by the government of Canada. It speaks eloquently of the need to be responsive to the elderly.

Special design considerations must figure strongly to compensate for . . . infirmities, if ease, comfort and dignity are to be attributes of old age. . . . Age doesn't seem to diminish the desire to be where the action is, and today, this is equally important to the elderly as it is to the young. . . . The National Housing Act, administered by Central Mortgage and Housing Corporation, offers loans at preferred interest rates to both private and public agencies willing to accept a limited or non-profit return from financial support of housing for the elderly. Designers, service clubs, church groups, private entrepreneurs and provincial and municipal housing organizations are invited to visit the manager of the nearest local Central Mortgage and Housing Corporation office and obtain information in financing senior citizen housing.

The corporation speaks of new housing developments, of senior citizen apartments or even communities. But where does it mention the most important need, namely, allowing the old to continue life in their own neighbourhoods, living in their own homes? To the organization charged with implementing so much of what may loosely be described as this nation's housing policy there is but a limited role for single-family housing. In the careful, self-protecting language of the bureaucracy the Central Mortgage and Housing Corporation states: "Current building practices favour small units either for a single person or for a husband and wife. Inevitably in the cases of the latter, the partnership is broken through death. In view of changing lifestyles and attitudes, perhaps the philosophy of single accommodation should be re-examined and alternatives reviewed to provide for greater flexibility.''

The thrust of the corporation is new housing, not the refurbishing of old housing. But the possibilities for such old housing are substantial. Mrs. Schramm would not have to vegetate in a senior citizens residence far from her neighbourhood. She need not be on welfare, in the sense of subsidized housing. She could contribute to the cost of maintaining a home fully owned by another older person. Neither Mrs. Schramm nor the elderly home owner would need the same degree of assistance from the social worker. Mrs. Schramm and the home owner could share not only household tasks but, just as important, they could bring each other into contact with the outside world. They need not suffer the kind of isolation which so often can destroy a person.

This human survival can be expressed in economic terms. The estimated cost for long-term bed facilities involving medical care can range as high as $40,000 for each bed. This does not include the very substantial government subsidy for such care which amounts to more than $6,000 annually for each recipient.

Are the statistics deceptive? After all, those receiving medical care are in need of some nursing each day. Maybe. But estimates made by one researcher who studied nursing homes in Montreal indicate that as many as half of those in such homes could be living in the community. For them, institutionalization is neither necessary nor desirable.

If the financial savings of keeping the elderly in their own homes are so dramatic, then why hasn't government launched a massive campaign to refurbish the housing owned by older persons? Why hasn't government encouraged the redesigning of such housing to include not only physical improvements such as ramps and hand rails, but also sharing occupancy with another person or family? Homes can be made into flexible shelter units. Just as Mrs. Schramm could move into a home, a young family could also do so. In fact, it would benefit them both: the older person or couple might be willing to help care for the children while the young couple work.

There are precedents for such flexible use of housing that will keep an older person vital and, at the same time, save substantial tax dollars. Unfortunately, on any large scale these precedents are not Canadian. But they exist in both the Western and the Communist worlds. For example, it has long been the custom in the Soviet Union for the older person, following retirement, to move into his or her children's apartment and care for the grandchildren. Such a move frees the young couple and also entitles them to a larger apartment.

More to the point perhaps is the national policy of Britain. There older people have a desire to maintain their homes. And the central government is responsive. It makes block grants available to county and local governments, which are used partly to improve old property. Cash grants go to older persons, to install ramps and hand rails. The old are not forced from their homes either by neglect or by what sometimes appears to be a misdirected sense of caring.

When a person moves to an institution he no longer has control of his own life. Nor is a surrender secret; it is negotiated, executed implemented before witnesses. It is not surprising that the high death rates among the old occur either among those who are on waiting lists for admission into nursing homes or homes for the aged, or shortly after their admission. (In some instances the rate can be as high as 30 to 50 per cent.) They have admitted their dependence, but are forced to wait in one world for admission into another.

> Individuals who are waiting to enter an old age home are psychologically "worse off" than those already in the institution. The characteristics that distinguish the waiting list group or the individuals already living in the institution include general anxiety and tension, high emotional reactivity, a sense of helplessness and powerlessness, a tone of depression accompanied by low self-esteem . . . an active withdrawal from those around them . . . A quality of "my life is over" permeates the waiting list group, a process likened to a "social death" with [similar] feelings of mourning.

The surrender of self to others is more than a paper surrender. The new controllers are well defined. They are the staff; they may be concerned for and even love the residents. Yet the staff live outside the home; they are present only during eight-hour shifts. More often than not they have uniforms to distinguish them and, more often than not, the uniforms are white, stressing the medical aspects of confinement and projecting the symbol of the residents' helplessness.

The staff know the lives of the residents intimately. But the residents know little about the personal lives of the staff. The staff can impinge and indeed, by statute and regulation, must impinge on the lives of the residents. Nighttime checks are required — in the interest of the resident. Medicine cannot be taken without a doctor's prescription and, in effect, the approval of the home. Residents cannot leave the home without notifying and, in some cases, obtaining the approval of the administrator. If the administrator considers it necessary, he or she is empowered to confine the resident to bed using restraining devices.

Residents may speak with the staff, but there can be little doubt that effective control has been taken from the self and given to others.

Bigger Institutions[3]

The lines were not always so well defined. In 1918, when the internationally known Baycrest Centre for Geriatric Care of Toronto was founded as an Old Folk's Home and before it became famous and big (it now shelters more than four hundred and fifty in its home for the aged), it housed about fifty old people in a small building, with a small resident professional staff.

For all of its newness, for all of its amenities, professional staff at the centre speak longingly of the days past when, so they believe, there was a closer relationship to the residents. Size alone, however, does not have to extract such a high price in distancing staff from residents. It is interesting that the Clarke Institute of Psychiatry in Toronto, another internationally known institution, requires its staff *not* to wear uniforms, so that they cannot be distinguished from the patients by their dress. And in Britain staff often have living quarters alongside residents. That is, they make their homes in the same place as the residents.

A large uniformed professional staff, living apart from residents and yet controlling them, creates a sense of institution, not of home. The staff may be known to the residents in one sense, but in another they remain custodial strangers.

This gap between staff and residents is not necessary. There can be a closer relationship; there can even be a crossover. Residents could be encouraged to take on the duties of staff. This can be done not only in terms of performing minor chores, but in the actual governance of the home. While some home managements have tried to involve residents, the attitudes and values that impel separation of custodian from resident are worth examining.

Mrs. Dorfman lived alone. She is an active person, but with the passing years she sensed a growing isolation. Friends had died; relatives had moved. She did not want to be alone and she did not want to give up her apartment. A social worker suggested membership in a day care centre. Three times a week a bus would take her from her apartment to the centre. There, others her own age would meet, eat and participate in activities under the supervision of a professional staff aided by volunteers.

Mrs. Dorfman agreed to try, and with the help of the social worker was admitted to membership in the day centre. Mrs. Dorfman thought of herself as a young 70-year-old. While she enjoyed some of the centre activities, her greatest pleasure came from helping other members who had difficulty helping themselves.

The centre volunteers looked on Mrs. Dorfman as one of them. They were pleased when she asked to be called Anna. The volunteers had some difficulty understanding why the staff had an unwritten rule that required centre members to be referred to only by their surnames, Mr. Jones or Mrs. Smith, while staff members were to be called only by their first names, Sally or Ruth. Nor did volunteers mind when Anna used the staff washroom because it was more pleasant than that of the residents. In fact, the volunteers welcomed the crossover by Anna. And it is fair to say that other members of the centre did not object. Anna was special; she had a sense of independence.

The professional staff, however, did object. They might be friendly; they might even consult with the members, but there was no doubt where control rested — and members knew it. There was a line of separation between staff and centre members, and that line was not to be crossed. The volunteers were instructed to refer to Mrs. Dorfman only by her surname, and to remind her that she was to use the facilities of the members and not those reserved for the staff. Mrs. Dorfman was to be told of the demarcation line in a "caring, but firm" manner. If Mrs. Dorfman insisted on crossing the line, the staff would feel required to terminate Mrs. Dorfman's membership. This would not only sentence her again to isolation, but if Mrs. Dorfman ever wanted to enter the home to which the centre was attached, she would find her way barred. She would have proved herself unable to function in a cooperative manner.

Mrs. Dorfman did not cross the line again. She became a cooperative person.

Mrs. Dorfman only entered a day centre; she did not commit herself to a home for the aged or a nursing home. Had she done so, she would have exchanged her one-bedroom apartment with kitchenette and bath for confinement. If she were lucky and rich she would have a room to herself, though her bathing facilities would have to be shared. Her meals would be prepared and served in a common dining room. If she were not rich and living in the wealthy province of Ontario — so long as she remained in reasonably good health — she might have to share her room only with from one to three others. If she were living in many other places throughout Canada, she would share her room with three others.

Against such a background, the Central Mortgage and Housing Corporation speaks of the need to create a "sense of home."

> Respect for the rights of the elderly to be masters in their own homes is a philosophical concept that can be translated into design and managerial terms . . . Each unit within a housing project together with the sum total of amenities and services becomes home to the occupant. The right to privacy, to decide on unit-sharing arrangements, the extent of voluntary participation in communal activities, and a voice in the administration of the project are synonymous with some of the attributes of ordinary home life and decisions made there . . . The aesthetics of external and internal appearance have their impact on the sense of feeling at home. Problems inherent in subduing or completely erasing an institutional atmosphere in large projects are formidable. There are no ready answers, but the creation of a non-institutional environment in these circumstances poses a real challenge to physical and social planners.

In its brochures Ontario picks up the theme of the Central Mortgage and Housing Corporation. In a glossy, widely distributed picture book titled, "Welcome to Your Homes," the minister of social and family services states: "Consider yourself at home in one of Ontario's Homes for the Aged . . . You will find a Home for the Aged a friendly and comfortable place to live. A real home, where you can enjoy your favourite pastimes in the company of good friends. A home where you will receive a measure of personal care suited to your needs. And you are assured of high standards in every Ontario Home for the Aged by the Department of Social and Family Services."

The brochure describes a resident's room, "your room." "Each home is designed with the idea that you will still have your individual tastes and need for privacy. This will most usually be a room with one or two beds in which you will have individual furnishings. In fact, in several Homes you can bring *some* of your own familiar furniture with you." The picture seems bright, even though the brochure is concerned only with homes for those who, on the whole, lack the means to enter a private nursing home.

A "Model" Nursing Home[4]

For those who can pay, the picture, according to a psychiatric social worker, might be even brighter. It is true that she writes about only one nursing home located in Scarborough, a borough of Toronto. But that home is owned by Extendicare Limited which operates twenty-two nursing centres throughout Canada, containing a total of 3,912 beds, whose corporate policy is to impose uniformly high standards on each centre.

The social worker describes the Scarborough building as eminently accessible for visitors while, at the same time, allowing residents the opportunity to visit the city. Facing a main public transportation line, it is U-shaped and consists of two storeys. The home is set on fairly spacious, well-tended grounds that make for pleasant strolls in all but the worst weather.

"Inside the building, the ambience is all brightness and cheer. Attractive colours of paint and wallpaper provide a very uninstitutional effect. Liberal use of graphic art relieves the monotony of corridor walls. The rooms boast floor carpeting and window drapes. Fresh floral displays add to the prevailing pleasantness of the decor."

The home contains seventy rooms, each with two beds. "One of these rooms has a double bed, as a favour for the married couple who occupy it. In rooms with more than one bed, wall dividers between them ensure complete privacy." Three of the rooms have four beds each, and three have single beds.

The residence is divided into units; groups of rooms constitute a unit. Each unit has bathtub and shower rooms, as well as a common lounge with its television set, record player, easy chairs and tables. A dining room accommodates about one hundred persons at a time.

The Scarborough home is among the best that Canada offers its older citizens who are institutionalized and represents "more the enlightened possibility than the actual practice of geriatric care across the nation." Yet what are the basic facts of this enlightened practice? Are residents confined in the sense of being denied space for privacy, space for themselves? What is the reality in this "good" facility? Most of the rooms hold two persons. They are given some measure of privacy by a wall divider. For the outsider, that may seem privacy enough. After all, the divider allows for a physical separation.

There are large common rooms where the resident can go to be alone or entertain. In any event, whether the home is private or public, personal privacy must be balanced against costs, which already have increased at an alarming rate. In 1960 the government expenditure on nursing homes amounted to $47 million. In 1971 that expenditure totalled $186 million, representing an increase of 296 per cent. Even so, can we afford to deprive older people of privacy? What do they themselves have to say?

In 1973, operating under a federal New Horizons grant and with the cooperation of the Ontario government, Associated Senior Executives of Canada surveyed thirty-five homes for the aged in Ontario. The homes ranged in size from 40 to 484 beds and were located in Toronto, Ottawa and Thunder Bay. Half were operated by municipalities, the remainder by charitable organizations. The report said:

> "Privacy" is a word which means different things to different people. There is physical privacy; there is also intellectual and spiritual privacy. As one person interviewed in our survey expressed it: "It is important that at our stage in life one have a place to go occasionally for a quiet cry in privacy." Whatever one's personal interpretation may be, privacy, in varying degrees, is essential to the maintenance of self-respect and human dignity. Our senior citizens, whether residing in Homes for the Aged or in other circumstances, are entitled to the fullest possible measure of their own concept of "privacy", independence, and human dignity. An understanding of this concept should be the overriding guideline for all who are involved in designing, building, managing and supporting our Homes for the Aged and all other programmes for Senior Citizens.

As a principle privacy can be accepted. Application of the principle may be another matter, and it is application that makes the difference, that allows the resident to affirm individual self-worth or forces a retreat into a dark world of alienation. The existence of privacy can be tested in very specific ways.

By its nature a home for the aged is a community. The community has rules. Indeed, there must be rules for the community to exist. In the context of the structure created from the rules community life develops . . . Yet where in that structure is the resident able to nurture a sense of self? Where is the resident able to say: "I am not simply a boarder at this nursing home. I am my own person. I have my own individuality. I am not here simply to wake up at a certain time, take prescribed medicines, eat breakfast in a common room, engage in planned recreation or exercise, and then rest."

What space is given over to the resident alone? Has the resident a single room, filled with personal furniture such as objects, pictures, mementos? Is there a room where he or she can go to reminisce, to think, to imagine? Can an institution by its very nature afford the smallest space to foster a sense of privacy? In an institutional setting space costs money, and the state has limited funds. In this situation and by present standards it would be unrealistic to allow each nursing home resident the equivalent of a small apartment. In a generous society it seems enough, according to the practice, to *work toward* a point where a resident can share a room with another.

In an institution it is also unrealistic to provide single rooms. Such single rooms as exist are used primarily for married couples. (And even this presents difficulties. In most nursing homes sex segregation is necessary because of shared washing and bathing facilities.)

The "four-bed room" does exist in most nursing homes and homes for the aged. The term alone cannot describe the effect of confinement on personal life. In their 1973 survey of homes for the aged, the Associated Senior Executives of Canada found:

> In many homes visited a considerable number of residents were accommodated in "4-bed rooms". From these came most of the dissatisfaction. The layout is generally standardized. Two beds are headed against each side wall, facing the opposite beds. Of necessity, two beds are on the window side, two on the interior side. A reasonably wide passage extends down the centre of the room, and space between side-by-side beds is generally sufficient. Each bed has a small bed-side chest and a light over the head of the bed operated, usually, by a pull cord.

How do four people, removed from their normal life in the community, function in a "four-bed room"? When space is so small and life so removed from the world outside, is it unreasonable to expect people to turn inward and grasp what little there may be, to claim territory, and assert minor prerogatives? The Associate Senior Executives reported on the problems of the "four-bed room":

— The occupants of the window-side beds tend to stake a personal claim to the window areas, the view, the use of the sills for flowers, plants and knick-knacks.
— Closets for all four occupants are along the inside wall. This requires the occupants of the window side to impinge on the "territory" of the inside beds in order to reach their closets.
— The room has two to four small, stiff chairs. There is no comfortable sitting area for four people.
— "Only in a few places are there divider curtains or screens.

Hence, there is no privacy at all for dressing or undressing.''
— ''In any group of four people there may well be at least one who
tends to be untidy, slovenly and careless about dress and personal
habits. This is irritating and a cause for dissatisfaction among
room-mates. . . . ''

The limitations of space extract still another price from the elderly
resident. He or she must leave behind the possessions and the furniture
of a lifetime. The demands of space, even the luxury of a two-bed room,
will permit under the most lenient administration only a few pieces of
furniture, only a few mementos.

The Associated Senior Executives of Canada stated: ''Some Homes
have strict rules that the resident must not bring any furniture from his or
her own home. Some allow a favourite picture or two only. Others
allow one to bring a favourite chair, a small chest or other piece so long
as they do not overcrowd the room or inconvenience the other
occupants. In single rooms a good deal of one's own furnishings can be
accepted. In two-bed rooms there are a few limitations . . . We favour
the most lenient policy consistent with [the] comfort of other occupants
of the room and with efficient housekeeping. Most residents interviewed favoured having a few things of their own, although many were
not interested.''

The law, however, is not overly concerned with privacy. Its primary
thrust is to achieve a more modest end, namely, safety. Nursing homes
and homes for the aged must be constructed of fire-resistant material;
corridors have to be sufficiently wide to allow for access; rooms must
have no locks so that residents can be checked.

This is not to say that the law's interest is constricted. In Ontario, for
example, nursing homes constructed before 1972 had to allow each
resident six hundred cubic feet of air space and seventy-five square feet
of floor space. Homes constructed after 1972 must allow somewhat
greater space. In charitable old age homes there is even more detail
about the use of miniscule space: beds are to be placed so that ''no bed
overlaps a window or radiator and no bed at any point is nearer to any
other bed than two and a half feet.''

The law has advanced a long way. Seventy years ago, homes for the
aged were called and were managed as ''houses of refuge.'' The safety
and security of residents were of no great concern to government.

It is fair to say that in the 1970s the safety and security of residents in
nursing homes and homes for the aged are the concern of government. It
is also fair to say that safety and security do not in themselves assure

quality of life. They do not bring privacy; they do not support a sense of self-worth.

The rooms described are not temporary quarters. They are not used for short-term hospital care. They may be lived in by the same person for fifteen, twenty, even thirty years. By 2001 there will be about 89,000 women and 27,500 men over 90. These are people who could have entered a home for senior citizens at the age of 65. Can the rooms they are allocated be called ''home''?

CHAPTER THREE

Point of No Return: Entering a Home

"Premature admission to an institution can kill, just as prescription of the wrong drug."

A Seller's Market: Standards for Admission[1]

There is no need to advertise. There are waiting lists for entrance into nursing homes and homes for the aged. Because the demand for beds is far greater than the supply, it is the home that dictates, subject to law, standards for admission. The applicant either must meet those standards or remain alone.

Whether the home is operated by government or "industry," with its concern for profit, all have a model applicant: (a person in reasonably good health, able to care for himself, yet needing a minimal amount of nursing care which can be provided by one who is not a registered nurse and generally is not even a registered nursing assistant. Finally, the applicant should have some prospect of living more than a few years following admission.

Mrs. Smythe is now 72 years old. Her children have long since moved from the city. She does not see them often, and, in any event, they have lives of their own to lead. For more than fifty years Mrs. Smythe's job, and it was one she loved, was that of wife and mother. A few years ago her husband died following a long and costly illness. The Smythes could best be described as a middle-income family. They owned their home, a small bungalow, possessed a few thousand dollars in a savings account, and Mr. Smythe had a modest life insurance policy and company pension. But her husband's illness, coupled with funeral expenses totalling about $1,500, left Mrs. Smythe with very little money. In fact, she had only just enough to maintain the home and provide for her needs.

More to the point, however, Mrs. Smythe became extremely depressed following her husband's death. Though she was in good physical health, she was also emotionally frail. Her few remaining friends worried about her and called a social work agency. A well-meaning and caring social worker, who thought she knew how to "fight the system" and could bend rules for a good cause, visited Mrs. Smythe.

The social worker saw in Mrs. Smythe a woman alone and in need of help. In her view, Mrs. Smythe ought to have others round her. Nearby was an Ontario government-operated home for the aged, where Mrs. Smythe would find other people her age and still be able to visit her remaining few friends.

Difficulties remained in gaining admission for Mrs. Smythe that she herself would never be able to overcome. The home would not accept applicants fully able to fend for themselves; on the other hand, it would not accept applicants in need of substantial care. The impasse arose from the standards for admission which are expressed with a certain deceptive simplicity. Homes for the aged in Ontario are permitted to admit any person:

— who is over the age of 60 and incapable of supporting himself or unable to care properly for himself; or
— who is over the age of 60 and mentally incompetent requiring care, supervision, and control for his protection, but not sufficiently incompetent to be placed in a psychiatric facility; or
— who is over the age of 60 requiring bed care and general personal nursing services, but not to such a degree that he could be admitted to a hospital.

Mrs. Smythe did not fit into any of these categories, but the social worker was enterprising. She found a friendly doctor who gave a medical opinion: Mrs. Smythe had just suffered an enormous personal trauma in the loss of her husband. While she was in good physical health, her condition was, in fact, precarious. He considered Mrs. Smythe fragile, and that the cumulative effect of loneliness, if allowed to continue, could break her.

Supported by this judgment, the social worker was able to depict Mrs. Smythe as a fragile, dependent person who, for the most part, could take care of herself in the setting of a home for the aged.

In one sense it can be said that the decision to enter the home was Mrs. Smythe's own. It was she who decided that her depression would not end by staying alone among the possessions and in the home where she had lived for so many years with her husband. The social worker only helped Mrs. Smythe to understand her position. The social worker only offered an option to loneliness. Mrs. Smythe exercised that option.

On the face of it, the choice of the home offered hope. Mrs. Smythe had read the government brochures with their large type and many pictures. Didn't they say, "Welcome To Your Home"? The brochures were most reassuring: "You will find a Home for the Aged a friendly and comfortable place to live. A real home, where you can enjoy your favourite pastimes in the company of good friends. A home where you will receive a measure of personal care suited to your needs. And you are assured of high standards in every Home for the Aged [operated by the provincial] Department of Social and Family Services."

The brochures implied, and the social worker stressed, that Mrs. Smythe need not worry about money. If she lacked the means to meet the cost of staying in the home, government would still give her the very best of its facilities. After all, a home for the aged was not a charitable institution where residents saw themselves as outcasts from society. As the administrator of a "model" home put it:

> The older person will walk into the institution, head upright . . . choosing to live there and not die there, and [we] should back up this expectation by asking him to show it to us by how he gets to participate and begin[s] to pick up the thread of his living within the institution. It means being ready to, aye ready, to tell him that there are plenty of holes in this world he can find to crawl into if he wished only for a place to die . . . It means expecting him to be helpful up to his capacity.

The social worker gave Mrs. Smythe hope. For being old, for not having wealth, she need not lose her pride. She would live among friends who cared for her and for whom she could care. She was encouraged to live fully, to participate in the community she was about to join, though she had not even visited the home itself.

Then came the forms. A welfare officer brought them. Though the officer was pleasant enough, and though Mrs. Smythe's "own" social worker was present, the forms greatly disturbed Mrs. Smythe. More than half of them concerned a "statement of income and assets." The information demanded was detailed and exhaustive; there were nineteen general questions to each of which were attached other queries. The welfare officer wanted a listing of all investments of stocks, bonds, mortgages, loans and life insurance, as well as other assets, together with *any transfers* of assets within the past three years. (This would include gifts to her children of any appreciable value.)

Then followed the questions concerning her home: a description of the property; its ownership; its assessed value; its present market value; the date of purchase; the purchase price; the nature of any encumbrances on the property; annual taxes; and any arrears of taxes.

All bank accounts had to be listed. This meant more than the name of the bank. It meant that Mrs. Smythe had to give her account number; the amount on deposit; and the date of the most recent withdrawal.

Moreover, she was required to identify her safety deposit box at the bank and where the key to that box was located.

The welfare officer went beyond Mrs. Smythe's own holdings. To determine their responsibility, she probed the financial standing of Mrs. Smythe's family. She asked questions and demanded answers concerning any money that Mrs. Smythe's children might have given her. The welfare officer asked in a nice but firm manner for the following information concerning the children:

— Their names
— Their addresses
— Their ages
— Their occupations
— Their marital status
— Whether they had children and, if so, how many
— The amount of any financial contribution to Ms. Smythe during the past year.

"But isn't this my decision? Why do my children have to be brought into this? I alone decided that I would enter the home. Why do you ask questions about how much money my children might have given me? Why are you concerned with how much money or property I might have?"

The welfare officer looked up from her work. She hoped that Mrs. Smythe would not become a problem. She liked her and did not want to indicate in her evaluation that Mrs. Smythe might be a stubborn person, prone to question the rules of the institution, and therefore not compatible with its environment.

Perhaps if she gave Mrs. Smythe a simple explanation she might more easily understand the purpose of all these questions. The welfare officer could then complete the form and recommend acceptance. "Try to understand me, Mrs. Smythe. The government really will provide you with a nice home. You should consider the home for the aged as your home. The government will also see to it that you have quite proper accommodation even if you do not have money to pay for it. Charity, however, is something that I am sure you do not want. What the government does is to require each person to pay what that person is able to pay. You understand that when you enter one of our homes it will be for the remainder of your life, unless, of course, you decide to leave.

"We will charge you for your stay in our home, and your property will be held in trust by us. On your death, or should you decide to leave us, we will place a charge on that property for your stay with us. "We will leave something — about $500 — aside for your funeral. In addition, we will see to it that every month a certain amount of pocket money will be given to you. You can figure that each month you will receive about $35 from us."

Mrs. Smythe sat quietly for a few minutes. The welfare officer and the social worker looked on patiently. In a subdued voice Mrs. Smythe asked: "Does the property that I must turn over to you include the pension I have been receiving since the death of my husband? Does it include the Old Age cheque from the government?"

"Yes, Mrs. Smythe. Both pensions must be turned over to us. But you will receive $35 a month. And remember we will be taking care of you. We will be providing you not only with room and board and services, but also friends. . . . Now please read this form and sign it. We want you to understand thoroughly what you are doing."

Mrs. Smythe did not want charity. She had thought that the taxes her husband had paid over the years might have provided a home without taking all she owned. The welfare officer had made it clear that this was not to be. With some hesitancy Mrs. Smythe signed the form, and in a short time became what might be described as a ward of the government.

At the rate of $200 to $500 a month, the cost for maintaining her at a home, it would not take long before the property held in trust would vanish. Nor did Mrs. Smythe have any false hopes that the home which she owned would be passed on to her children following her death. The government would first take Mrs. Smythe's liquid assets in payment for her maintenance. Then, if more were owed, following her death, the government would levy upon her home, which would be seized and sold by auction to satisfy the debt to the government. The Ontario High Court enforced this power as recently as 1973.

The Meaning of Admission: Unspoken Fears[2]

In at least two ways Mrs. Smythe was fortunate. The welfare officer knew this, but she did not want to confuse further an already traumatized person. Mrs. Smythe really understood what she was doing; she wanted to enter the home. The welfare officer knew that there were many who did not fully comprehend their decision. It is possible for a person to be admitted to a nursing home or a government-run facility without consent, induced by family, physician or social workers to seek admission. The law, as such, imposes no rigorous standard. It is true that in Ontario, for example, regulations require that "a person shall not be admitted as a resident [to a nursing home] without his consent, the consent of his next of kin or legal representative," and government-run homes (homes for the aged) require applicants to sign their requests for admission. Further, Mrs. Smythe was fortunate that her children were not compelled to pay any portion of the cost for maintaining their mother even though enquiries had been made. Again the welfare officer knew that many homes require the children to pay either all or a portion of the cost for maintaining a parent. At the Baycrest Centre for Geriatric Care in Toronto fully one-third of the residents in the home pay the full amount of $600 per month for maintenance. This amount, in turn, is provided directly or indirectly, wholly or partly, by the residents' children. The welfare worker was well aware that the government could *force* children to support their parents. Such is the law. But the law was not being enforced.

The difficulty is just what the procedures for admission really mean. While government has imposed a consent standard on nursing homes, the same government has prescribed no means for implementing it. No consent form is required, and there is no regularly scheduled investigation or inspection to determine compliance with the standard.

"Why should we prescribe forms? Why should we investigate or inspect to ensure complaince with a generalized standard of consent? After all, entry into a nursing home is a matter of contract, just as entry into a government-run home is a matter of agreement. No one is *committed*, as such, to a nursing home or home for the aged. Once admitted, a resident is always free to leave. Remember we are not out seeking residents. There are more people wanting beds than there are beds." Such is the rationale of government (and the nursing home industry).

But it is not true that residents are free to leave the home. Once they enter, they have no choice. Their money is placed in a special account, and within a few years will all have been spent on the costs of institutional maintenance. Then what happens to the resident wanting to leave? Penniless, perhaps even owing money to the institution, how is he or she to assert his or her independence? In some respects, it might even be said that the system motivates the resident to die sooner rather than later. After all, the sooner he or she dies, the less the estate will be encumbered. To live in a home for many years is to be increasingly dependent on the institution.

Financial dependence is just *one* aspect of life in an institution. An emotional dependence, which can be encouraged, also exists because of the employees whose function it is to serve and care for residents. Mrs. Meyer is a nursing home resident. With encouragement, with some assistance and patience, Mrs. Meyer could take care of her portion of the room. She could make her bed, though not with hospital neatness. (And, there might even be a few times when she might forget to fix the bed.) She could tidy her room, given the time and equipment for doing so. Yet, obviously, it would take Mrs. Meyer much longer to manage than a nursing assistant or practical nurse. Mrs. Meyer could also fix many of her own meals. But the home cares for more than sixty residents; it cannot allow these residents to enter and make free use of the kitchen. Moreover, there is no assurance that Mrs. Meyer or other residents would feed themselves properly. It is much easier for the institution to ensure that Mrs. Meyer is cared for fully by a trained staff. With this caring comes dependence.

The staff psychiatrist for the Maimonides Hospital and Home for the Aged in Montreal wrote:

> It has been extremely difficult to introduce the concept of self-determination and self-reliance. Suggestions by residents, when practical, were implemented. However, any attempts at self-care — e.g. the establishment of a welcoming committee to introduce new residents to the floor, or a dietary committee to help in meal planning and to deal with complaints — always met with resident resistance and failed. After three years of ward meetings, we have been able to motivate a few patients to help the nursing staff actively and take some responsibility for their own welfare. *The resistance cannot be assigned wholly to the patients; nurses, aides and orderlies often resisted change. It is easier to minister to the needs of aged and infirm patients than to provide the leadership to overcome their regression, anger and passivity.*

For the resident there is no choice but to remain in the home, but there is no assurance that the home will maintain the resident till death. On October 8, 1972, the Toronto *Globe and Mail* published a letter from a physician. His uncle had been sent from a nursing home to a hospital because the home did not have the facilities necessary for treatment. The uncle stayed in the hospital for more than three days. As a result, the nursing home dismissed him, and gave his bed to a new resident. The physician had to find another home for his uncle. Why, the physician asked, should his uncle have lost his bed, his home? Didn't the nursing home understand that a move at this point was an emotional shock to the old man?

The nursing home did understand. Surely, however, the physician must know that the nursing home, indeed any nursing home, could not *guarantee* in all circumstances a place for a resident. Wasn't it enough, the nursing home answered, as a matter of practice (though not required by law), that the resident was given seven days' notice of the home's intent to discharge him? As seen by government, nursing homes, like homes for the aged, are not hospitals, only links in the health care chain.

A very large percentage of hospital patients are elderly persons. Moreover, their stay in hospitals is often lengthy and they take up costly bed space. Government policy has been to remove as many of the elderly from hospitals as possible, which was done by targeting in upon those of the elderly requiring limited medical attention.

The government accordingly devised the concept of extended care. In Ontario extended care is that "required by a person with a relatively stabilized disease or disability who has reached the apparent limit of recovery and is not likely to change in the near future." In addition, this person must have "relatively little need for the diagnostic and therapeutic services of a hospital while still requiring the availability of personal care on a continuing 24-hour basis with medical and nursing supervision and provision for meeting psycho-social needs. The period of time during which care is required is unpredictable but usually consists of a matter of months or years." With greater or lesser refinement, the Ontario definition is one used throughout Canada and the United States.

Rather than providing subsidies for hospital beds that could amount to between $100 and $150 per day in 1977, government gives nursing homes subsidies of $13.60 per day (supplemented by the patient) for each extended care bed. (Government then made sure that there would be a pool of extended care beds by requiring nursing homes to have a given percentage of their total bed space equipped for extended care.)

Yet extended care is a most limited kind of medical attention. In Ontario the law stipulates a minimum of ninety minutes of skilled nursing care each day. This does not require the services of a registered nurse. *At best*, it is generally provided by a registered nursing assistant, who has far less training.

Nursing homes rely upon the government subsidy for each patient, which comes only if extended care is given. Moreover, nursing homes are not hospitals. Should a resident require full-blown medical services, the nursing home has little choice but to remove the resident to a hospital. Once the patient has left the home, the empty bed will not bring the government subsidy, for after seventy-two hours extended care is no longer given. The home is a private enterprise; it is run for profit, and the owners are under pressure to fill the empty bed or see their profits diminish. In cold economic terms, where the mortality rate in some nursing homes is as high as 30 per cent each year, the pressure to fill beds is significant. It must be added that the pressure in government-run homes to fill empty beds is also great. In the language of economists, empty beds reflect underutilized space. Government, like the private sector, establishes budgets in relation to services rendered.

The problem is not so much a question of the profit motive as against government ownership, but rather the nature of the government subsidy which is given for extended care as a link in the medical care chain. Action by nursing home and old age home managements must be related to the subsidy. So change the rules, make it available to the resident, and nursing home management's actions will change accordingly. In other words, assume for a moment that Mrs. Smythe received the Ontario subsidy directly for as long as she lived. Would she have the same fear of losing her space in the nursing home? In accordance with the profit motive, wouldn't the nursing home be directed to serve Mrs. Smythe? But as long as the subsidy comes to the institution, not the individual, Mrs. Smythe knows from the beginning that the home she enters is hers only so long as her "condition remains stable."

For its incoming residents the Baycrest Centre for Geriatric Care has a Code of Admission. The code is pleasantly worded, but its meaning is beyond cavil: "Continued need for the type of care the Home provides: The resident shall be deemed not to need the Home when the mental deterioration is of such a degree that he is not in contact with the environment and therefore derives no particular benefit from being in the Home, as differentiated from other care which may be available to him."

Now, what one matter concerns older people more than any other? The fear of becoming sick and not being able to care for themselves. For a resident in a nursing home that anxiety can be especially great because sickness means the potential loss of home, money and independence.

Becoming sick and being displaced is not the only fear. What will happen if the home closes? There is no real danger that a government-run home will ever be closed, but a private one is a different matter. In Ontario a total of 118 nursing homes have closed since 1972. Of these, 108 voluntarily surrendered their licences, 50 of which occurred since 1974. A total of ten closings were the result of sanctions imposed by government. Eight of these took place before 1974 and two after 1974. Neither nursing homes nor homes for the aged are required by law, nor is it their general practice to mention to applicants the contingencies that could result in loss of home and care.

The essential point is that the government cannot stop a nursing home from going out of business nor can it prevent a home from closing. And nursing homes will close voluntarily if they find that the regulations for operation are too stringent and the profit margin too narrow. As recently as April 23, 1976 the Ottawa *Journal* reported that MacLaren House, a nursing home for one hundred residents, was for sale, partly as a result of government enforcement of regulations. The government would not prohibit the sale or the closing. What the government would do was ensure alternative accommodation for the one hundred residents.

A representative of the Ontario Ministry of Health said: "There is no way that we will close down a nursing home without adequate notice to residents and relatives and certainly not before we can provide them with alternative facilities for care." The place that was home for one hundred people would be no more. At best they would be severed from their community, from their home, and parcelled out to new quarters to make new adjustments. The resident has no voice in the closing of a nursing home, only the right of "alternative facilities."

To the residents, the continued existence of the home and its facilities are important matters. But in no small measure a home is not just a building, but also the people who staff it and care for the residents. Work in nursing homes cannot be called the most attractive of jobs. Union officials estimate the turnover rate among employees *in any one year* to be as high as 30 to 50 per cent. It is altogether possible that the people caring for residents would not really know them because they would not be there long enough.

Yet what of the basic promise of continuous care? Can the nursing home and the home for the aged ensure it? Although government might prohibit strikes by employees in nursing homes, the law cannot fully govern behaviour. For example, in 1974 at the Hearst Nursing Home in Ontario sixty-one infirm patients were left alone for three hours as twenty employees, including registered nursing assistants, staged a wildcat strike. The residents, who could not fend for themselves, had to be moved to other nursing homes. Many appeared later at hospital in clothes stained with food because they had tried to cook for themselves. Government could not stop the wildcat strike; it could only prosecute after the event — after the damage had been done.

Can it be said that gaining admission to a home will make it be a resident's until death? Can it be said that the quality of care will remain at a constant level without interruption until death? Above all, can it be said that applicants to nursing homes and homes for the aged really understand what kind of home they are entering?

No nursing home or homes for the aged have even begun to initiate the limited effort made by the Ontario Hospital Association (OHA) to develop and publicize a "philosophy of patient care." The OHA programme is a limited undertaking, designed to encourage member hospitals to develop a concise, readable statement of rights, responsibilities, and expectations of patients, hospital and staff all of whom are expected to contribute their opinions. The statement, once formulated, is to be distributed widely so that new patients and the community at large can accept their responsibilities and have a better understanding of hospital services.

The OHA Board of Directors stated:

It is important that those concerned with providing hospital care recognize that the growth of "consumerism", the increased speed of communication, and a rise in the general level of education are producing a more informed and less passive patient.

The time is now past when a patient will accept without question or complaint the treatment he or she is given in hospital. Today, administrators can expect questioning, complaints and criticism as well as the occasional lawsuit if a patient feels, rightly or wrongly, he or she has not received satisfactory treatment.

Almost always such situations arise from a lack of communication or a misunderstanding between one or more of the people or groups of people involved: the hospital and its staff, the physician(s), and the patient and his or her family.

Members of the general public are unfamiliar with the organization of the hospital. Most take the hospital for granted until they need its services. At that time, the patient may enter hospital with expectations and assumptions that are, perhaps, unreasonable. He or she may be confused about "rights" and unaware of responsibilities.

The OHA Public Relations Committee, through its Subcommittee on Patient Relations, identified a need for a short, simply-written document which outlines the aims, methods of operation and philosophy of the hospital for the benefit of patients, hospital employees, medical staff, and the community at large.

Why cannot nursing homes and homes for the aged formulate a similar statement of rights and responsibilities which applicants for admission can understand and evaluate before they enter the home? In today's so-called consumer society, products must be labelled. If a product is potentially dangerous, special warnings are required. Some drugs can be purchased only by prescription. Why should not services, or the absence of services, also be labelled?

The analogy to prescription drugs can be carried further. A consumer might very much want a particular drug, but that desire alone will not permit purchase. The state charges a qualified person, generally a physician, with making a professional determination: for better health, does the patient need the drug? Other than the "extended care" qualification, there are no controls imposed on nursing homes; they may accept whomever they so desire. And, on balance, the only controls operating on government-run homes is that the applicant be of a certain age, have some need which the home can meet, and, in the context of that need, be otherwise able to function normally.

There really are no objective and professional judgments on whether the applicant for the home could function as well if not better in the community. All too often social workers and physicians become emotionally involved with the applicant and use their talents to develop the arguments which will allow the older person to enter the home.

Dr. H. Grauer, senior psychiatrist, Jewish General Hospital, Montreal writes:

> Admission to an institution may be prompted by a life crisis and by pressure from relatives, the patient's physician or police officers. The decision to place a patient is often left in the hands of inexperienced professionals. However, (it has been found) that, even if trained professionals are employed, institutional placement and morbidity (death) occur sooner and more frequently in a group receiving "professional social work services" than in a matched group receiving few or no social services. *The explanation could be that even an experienced professional sometimes is influenced by emotional bias to institutionalize patients prematurely.*

Dr. Grauer argues for an objective rating scale to determine the need for institutional care, and he has developed one that combines the assessment of physical and mental disability with the assessment of ability to function. It also takes into account such factors as financial support from relatives and friends. (Such support becomes important not in terms of contributing to the cost of maintaining the applicant in the home for the aged, but rather as an affirmative factor in keeping him or her in the community.)

Dr. Grauer's rating scale also considers the availability of community resources such as recreational facilities and meals-on-wheels. "In this fashion," he says, "we are able to make a global assessment of a person's ability to maintain himself in the community. . . . . Physical and mental disability are given minus values; the ability to function and the support measures are given plus values." The scale attempts to eliminate, as far as possible, abstract, subjective judgments as the primary basis for resolving the question of entry into a home. Points are awarded under particular headings, so that, within a range, judgments concerning admission can be made.

Dr. Grauer makes the point that others have often made: premature admission to an institution can kill.

Carmelita Lester agrees with Dr. Grauer. Ms. Lester, a native of the West Indies, arrived in North America in 1962 and has worked as a practical nurse in nursing homes for five years. As quoted by Studs Terkel in *Working*, she says:

> In [North] America, people doesn't keep their old people at home. At a certain age they put them away in [North] America. In my country, the old people stay in the home until they die. But here, not like that. It's surprising to me. They put them away. The first thing they think of is a nursing home. Some of these people don't need a nursing home. If they have their own bedroom at home, look at television or listen to the radio or they have themselves busy knitting. . . . We all, us foreigners, think about it.
> Right now there's a lady here, nothing wrong with her, but they put her here anyway. They don't come to see her. The only time they see her is when she say, "I can't breathe". She wants some attention. And that way she's just aging. When I come here, she was so beautiful. She was looking very nice. Now she is going down. If they would come and take her out sometimes . . . all these people here are not helpless. But the family get rid of them.

CHAPTER FOUR

Life in the "Home": Confinement

The fear of a prisoner is that there will be delay in release from the institution. The fear of a resident in a home for the aged is that there will be release into the community.

Loneliness: The Lost Person[1]

What can the social worker or the welfare officer say to applicants about life in the "home"? They can at best tell only a portion of the story since neither the social worker nor the welfare officer nor, for that matter, any employee of the home lives there. They are not confined to the institution twenty-four hours a day for the remainder of their lives. As employees, what can they really understand of the residents' feelings?

It is not easy for residents to speak. Sometimes, however, they express their full feelings. Not long ago a poem was found in the bed locker of an old woman who died at a nursing home. The poem is harsh in its reality and tender in its feeling.

> What do you see nurses, what
>   do you see?
> Are you thinking when you are
>   looking at me
> A crabby old woman, not very
>   wise
> Uncertain of habit, with far
>   away eyes.
> Who dribbles her food and makes
>   no reply
> When you say in a loud voice, "I
>   do wish you'd try."
> Who seems not to notice the
>   things that you do
> And forever is losing a stocking
>   or shoe,
> Who, unresisting or not, lets you
>   do as you will

With bathing and feeding, the
  long day to fill
Is that what you're thinking? Is
  that what you see?
I'll tell you who I am as I sit here
  so still
As I use at your bidding, as I eat
  at your will.
I'm a small child of ten with a
  father and mother,
Brothers and sisters who love
  one another.
A young girl of sixteen with
  wings on her feet
Dreaming that soon now a lover
  she'll meet.
A bride soon at twenty, my heart
  gives a leap,
Remembering the vows that I
  promised to keep.
At twenty-five now I have young
  of my own
Who need me to build a secure,
  happy home.
A woman of thirty, my young
  now grow fast,
Bound to each other with ties
  that should last.
At forty, my young sons now
  grown will be gone
But my man stays beside me to
  see I don't mourn.
At fifty, once more babies play
  'round my knee,
Again we know children, my
  loved one and me.
Dark days are upon me, my
  husband is dead.
I look to the future, I shudder
  with dread.
For my young are all busy rearing
  young of their own,
And I think of the years and the
  love that I've known.

I'm an old woman now and nature
is cruel,
'Tis her jest to make old age look
like a fool.
The body it crumbles, grace and
vigor depart,
There is now a stone where I
once had a heart.
But inside this old carcass a
young girl still dwells,
And now and again my battered
heart swells.
I remember the joys, I remember
the pain,
And I'm loving and living life all
over again.
And I think of the years all too
few — gone too fast
And accept the stark fact that
nothing will last.
So open your eyes nurses, open
and see,
Not a crabby old woman, look
closer — see me!

This old woman is not alone in her loneliness. Doris Clark, a social worker, writes a widely syndicated column, "Successful Living," designed to interpret to the public what social work can do. For years she has encouraged elderly readers of her column to consider "with equanimity the prospect of life in a 'home-away-from-home.' [I have] extolled the advantages of spending enjoyable days among contemporaries with interests and memories in common." Then Ms. Clark began to have doubts fuelled by letters from residents in nursing homes. The first letter that follows is from a woman, the second from a man:

Living in a nursing home is perilous living . . . the thing is the loneliness. You can't make a good friend in a nursing home because you can't be sure. When you first go into a nursing home you are so very ready to be friendly. Yet you are suspected. If someone approaches you in the corridor you are ready with a . . . smile, but you meet a turned head or averted eyes. . . . Suddenly you realize they are not sure whether you are unstable or not. One dare not confide in the nursing aides. These people are so subject to rivalry among themselves for favour with their superiors that any personal confidences offered, or any questions concerning the rules, food, or personnel of the nursing home could quickly backfire. . . . Two women, both sadly senile, have walked in on me and have had to be literally carried out screaming, kicking and pinching the attendants. How I would love a bolt on my door! These, and the lack of any imagination regarding food, are the negatives in nursing homes. There are, I freely admit, many positives: medical supervision, comfort for the body, shelter within, the nicely kept grounds without. *But so little for the mind!*

The man lives in a nursing home in a completely different part of Canada:

One does not care so much about the physical assets of life — takes them for granted. It is the mental cruelty in our institutions that is so heartbreaking. On Christmas day I asked for someone to help me dress, as I cannot do this properly myself. I had my old neighbors coming to visit. . . . Someone laid a pair of pants beside me, which I was still contemplating when my visitors arrived. What a pretty picture I must have looked. . . . But what really hurt me deeply was the nurse's refusal to let me see my beloved dog, a 12-year-old collie. The dog would not have met any other guests, coming in a nearby door. The head nurses here make sure that their unlimited authority is forced on us. There is no practical reason for this behaviour except utter disregard for our feelings. *They know we cannot fight back*. Outside my room I hear patients cry for attention all day long. The other day I had an agitated lady, who was scared out of her wits because she overheard the nurses talking about "those crazy people", telling me she is not crazy yet she will surely lose her mind, staying here for any length of time, wishing to be dead. . . . Every little pleasure is systematically killed. One does not have anything more to look forward to than food (which is very good) and the fight against the body's weakness.

Yet there are nursing homes and homes for the aged which, as a matter of policy, do want to reach the resident and touch that person's life. The Maimonides Home for the Aged in Montreal is such an institution. From 1969 to 1971 the home experimented with the concept of a "therapeutic community." The concept itself is not overly complex. It accepts the fact that the home is a community where residents live and staff work. Let both groups come together and freely exchange feelings. The object of the exercise is mainly to allow individuals to see the effect of their own actions on others and through such insight judge their own behaviour.

The therapeutic community has been used with marked success in schools, prisons and mental hospitals. Senior staff at Maimonides knew, however, that its use in a home for the aged would meet with special problems:

— A home for the aged is different from a school, or prison, or mental institution. The residents of the home know that they will never leave; they are confined until death.
— A home for the aged is different in still another respect. In a school, or prison, or mental institution the individual can assist the professional staff. Indeed, the longer the student or inmate remains in the institution the more likely it is that the person can take on a trustee's duties. In a home for the aged there is a clear distinction between the staff and the residents. Moreover, the longer the resident stays at the home, the more likely that person is to be dependent and in need of greater care.

Still, Maimonides, under the supervision of a psychiatrist, experimented with the therapeutic community. Three times a week professional and non-professional staff serving about seventy residents of a particular floor of the home were brought together with those residents for a full exchange of feelings. Each meeting lasted for forty-five minutes and was followed by a staff meeting of thirty minutes. Arrangements were made with the home administration for summaries of the meetings at appropriate times.

What Maimonides did few nursing homes and homes for the aged have attempted. The staff hoped that those making up the home could build an environment and a way of living of benefit to all. Experimentation with the therapeutic community was another step toward establishing a sense of a quality of life. (At Maimonides the safety and physical well-being of residents are more than adequate.)

The experiment at Maimonides, however, at best can be called a marginal success. Only about a third of the residents regularly attended meetings — even when those meetings were held in an open area where the residents generally congregated. Of those who did attend, only about ten regularly participated in discussion.

Why did so few come? Sickness and anti-social behaviour were the reasons given. There was some thought of imposing sanctions on those who absented themselves from the group meetings; of expulsion from the home, but this was abandoned as too harmful to the resident.

The administration wanted to use the meetings as a means of involving the residents; after all, this was their home. So a rule was adopted that all complaints had to be brought before the meeting or else they would not be considered. The resident was no longer able to bring complaints to a favourite individual.

Forcing complaints before the group helped to increase attendance and stimulate discussion. Can it be said, however, that life in the home changed as a result? Did "open" discussion of grievances bring greater understanding and more sensitivity to individual needs? On balance, the quality of life in the home did not change. Nor can it be said that there was significantly greater understanding and sensitivity to individual needs. The staff and residents, however, did demonstrate a better awareness of the institutional facts of life, that is, both groups were able to grasp the rules that governed living in the home: the staff was there to care for the residents, the residents were there to receive care. This did not mean that one group could not influence another, nor did it mean that all within a group were treated in precisely the same way.

In the home was a clique of "veteran" residents, whose position as veterans gave them a special status which they used. They could and did with some frequency intimidate and anger other residents and junior staff members. The group meetings did not result in the elimination of the ruling clique. On the other hand, the supervising psychiatrist at the group meetings wrote that the veteran residents "often provided leadership and had positive persuasive power. The [group meetings] afforded everyone the opportunity to analyze and understand the hierarchy and to make their leadership more positive and less destructive to the group."

It may be that the group meetings softened somewhat the destructive edge of the veteran clique. There was, however, no radical change of direction. The clique continued to assert its power to the detriment of newcomers. Efforts by the staff to have the veterans establish a welcoming committee for new residents were turned down, as well as attempts to establish a committee concerned with planning meals. These were both areas where the clique enjoyed status. The clique "knew" the home and was able to obtain the food its members wanted.

The clique had another source of power which was probably more terrifying. It could "scapegoat" residents. That is, the clique could label another resident as "crazy" and the label would stick, with the result that the "crazy" person would be isolated, mocked, and become a sure instrument of demonstrating where power existed in the hierarchy.

Scapegoating did not end with the group meetings. Better understanding, however, resulted from discussions in which the clique, the staff and the "scapegoat" participated. The supervising psychiatrist wrote:

In the past, certain patients were "scapegoated" by fellow residents and the staff on the floor. Just as in a disturbed family, "craziness" was assigned to certain patients. This displacement and projection enabled the others to maintain the role of good and obedient children. The scapegoated patients were often driven to antisocial behaviour; thus verbal and physical fights were not infrequent, and these patients had to be referred to social service or the psychiatrist. This referral was often regarded as punitive, and it made therapeutic intervention extremely difficult. By taking up the problem of the disturbed patient in the group, preferably in his presence, mutual understanding often could be reached. This resulted in better handling of "difficult" residents by fellow patients and staff.

On the whole, then, the Maimonides residents did not see the council as a way to express themselves as individuals. After all, the council was not a mechanism to change the institution but a means for both staff and residents to accommodate themselves to it. After three years of experimentation the groups remained well defined. Nothing could change, for the residents would never leave the home except to die. This is not to deny the value of accommodation. If residents can accept their condition, then perhaps they will be able to find whatever happiness reality permits. If they reflect less on the past when they had their own homes and their own friends — now a fantasy world — and stop comparing it with the present, they will have a better chance of coming to terms with the present.

Of Prisons and "Homes": An Analogy[2]

Councils can involve residents. Many of Ontario's homes for the aged have residents' (councils which allow them some voice in the management of the home. For example, the residents of Dorchester Manor wanted to do their own laundry. The council framed a resolution which it presented to the administration. Within three weeks a washing machine and dryer were installed. The tradition of the administration, part of the Niagara municipal home system, is to encourage residents to participate inside and outside the home. Estimates are that 89 per cent of residents in Niagara homes attend some form of outside activity such as bowling, billiards, dancing or miniature golf tournaments.

Such councils, however, operate within the framework of the institution. To the extent that councils make residents feel comfortable they can be said to be effective. To the extent that councils challenge authority in any fundamental way they can be said to be dangerous to the well-being of both residents and institution.

Over the years, residents' councils have been singularly docile. Residents have not used them to challenge administration. Mild suggestions, not demands, surface from the councils. It is curious to compare an old age "facility" to a prison. The state maintains both as residences for an inmate population, and in a practical sense the resident of an old age home is no more free to leave that home than a prisoner is free to leave a prison. But the fear of a prisoner is that there will be delay in release from the institution. The fear of the resident in a home for the aged is that there will be release into the community. In their regulated lives the prisoner and the resident of the old age home are alike.

But then the similarity ends. Time after time in Canada and the United States, prisoners in both minimum and high security facilities have rioted, held their keepers captive, and even destroyed large parts of the prisons in which they lived. They have done this because they wanted their lives to be something more than the passing of time in terrible boredom all too often overlaid by custodial oppression.

With the prisoners' violence came public response. Committees of investigation were established, and their findings are relevant to old age homes. The Alberta Inquiry into the Alleged Excessive Use of Force at the Calgary Correctional Institute gave its report on August 23, 1973. It stated:

> Confinement of human beings against their will in close proximity to each other creates an abnormal and explosive situation. Trivial incidents take on a monumental significance. Frustration and violence are the norm and perversion is accepted. . . .
> The Commission concludes that in a custodial institution, *the provision of meaningful work is essential to reduce and bring within control the level of tension and frustration which incarceration inevitably produces. The attainment of this objective is not to be taken as a substitute for rehabilitation.* If the provision of such work demands greater expenditure on custodial capacity to control inmates while such work is carried on outside the secure portions of the institution, such expenditures must be made. . .The objectives of the concept of rehabilitation cannot be met within the custodial environment. All that can be hoped for in the custodial environment is that the inmate can be taught to live in that environment. It is rehabilitation which teaches him to live in society.

In September 1973 the government of Ontario sponsored its first Residents' Councils Conference for those in its homes for the aged. The government's words sounded the call for collective decision-making:

"These councils must be accepted by residents and staff as integral decision-making bodies within the homes. This requires that residents, as well as administrators and staff members, regard the councils as having authority to speak and decide on behalf of other residents."

As the conference proceeded these words took on a more precise meaning. Residents' councils were not meant to reorder the home. They were to allow life in the home to proceed smoothly. The conference concentrated on recommendations that had little to do with the quality of life. The resolutions, for example, struck at the "charitable" label given homes for the aged and asked that they be made to look more like individual residences, like "senior citizen" housing. The delegates to the conference were all too familiar with the stigma that still marked homes for elderly people, even though the bad old days of "houses of refuge" were long past.

Suggestions and changes in an institution for the elderly come slowly and gently. Administrators cannot be hurried. The life of the resident, however, remains the same, without much room for individual choice. There is a time for rising and a time for sleeping. Between 7:00 A.M. and 7:30 A.M. everyone has to get up, wash and dress. Breakfast is served between 8:00 and 8:30 A.M., and a resident cannot say that he or she would like to "sleep in" and breakfast later. An individual's wishes cannot be met, not that the staff or the administration in any overt sense is cruel, but life in an institution forces surrender of individual choice.

Surrender of Choice[3]

However much administration would like to vary the menu, the fact remains that there can be only limited choice. The home, public or private, has a fixed amount budgeted for food. If there are a hundred residents, it is unreasonable to expect each one's needs to be catered for except for those on diets prescribed by doctors. As well as lack of money, there is neither the staff nor the time to do so. The institution must operate for the benefit of all the residents.

Economies of scale impose a delicate balance between budgetary restraint and individual need. A budget forces government to fix priorities, to establish a programme. (Without a programme government cannot assess how effectively tax moneys are being used.)

For institutional care the government has a clearly defined programme. In its broad objectives it is designed to provide under humane conditions for the physical needs of the elderly. Practically, this means (treating those who enter institutions for the aged as a group, not as individuals. All within the group must receive (a nutritious diet, and the rules about this are detailed and precise. Institutions are expected, indeed they are required as a condition of licensing, to conform to the diet and nutrition rules of government.

What practical choice does an institution have but to design relatively simple menus that meet the requirements of government? Accordingly, breakfast consists of an egg, on occasion sausage, hot or cold cereal, toast, juice, coffee, tea or milk. Lunch is a sandwich, fruit salad or soup, sometimes a hot meal: casserole, dessert, bread and butter and a beverage. Supper, the main meal of the day, consists generally of meat, vegetables, potatoes, salad, bread and butter, dessert and beverage. Meals have to be served in an attractive manner. As happened at one nursing home that violated the regulations in Ontario, food must not be puréed, placed in a bowl, and handed to the resident to eat with a spoon. Regulations also provide for snacks, such as cookies and juice, at least once a day.

The regulations, to the extent that rules can do so, allow good homes to respond to individual needs and tastes. At best, however, institutional regulations can allow only a gesture to be made to the individual. The (fact remains that order, not individuality, must be the rule. Residents may be permitted to have some snacks in their rooms (such as candy or cookies) which they have purchased with their own money. But they will be "(positively discouraged" from having meals in their rooms either alone or with one or two friends. An institutional representative said: "If one resident wanted to eat in her room, then others might have the same desire. There simply is not enough staff to provide that kind of service." The staffs can rationalize their actions and explain why compulsory dining is for the benefit of residents: mealtimes encourage residents to be ambulatory, and are opportunities for socialization.

Suppose, however, that a residents' council recommends that at least once every two weeks residents be permitted to order special food from neighbourhood take-out restaurants. According to the recommendation, the residents could eat the food in their own room either alone or with friends. Moreover, bearing in mind "budgetary constraints," the residents' council asks that no more money be allowed each resident than is allocated each person for group meals. Would the institution approve the recommendation? Would the institution allow residents to order a pizza or a Chinese dinner? Can it be argued that the residents would be less ambulatory, that they would be less encouraged to know and be known by the community in which they live? Indeed, wouldn't the local take-out restaurants make some special effort to cater to steady business?

The likelihood is that the proposal for variation in menu would be discouraged. And the institution could offer an easy justification: (1) Government requires daily nutritional levels and a pizza or a Chinese dinner does not meet the required minimum standard. The institution must act for the benefit of residents even if residents don't understand what is in their best interests. (2) The home has no control over the quality of take-out food. The dinners might be too spicy for some residents, who get indigestion or stomach upsets. The institution controls its food; it provides a balanced diet and ensures cooking that will fit the resident's constitution. The institution, after all, bears a responsibility in law for the physical well-being of those committed to its charge. (3) To allow residents the right to order their own meals only once every two weeks would be disruptive to the staff. Special dining facilities might be required. Special arrangements might have to be made to clean up following the meal. (4) Perhaps most important, if the fortnightly dinners were a success, there might be a demand for more frequent take-out dinners, and this would disrupt the institution.

As things are, the institution will still be standing long after any one resident, any one administrator or any one staff member has left. The institution is a place where every newcomer — whether resident, administrator or staff member — can understand his or her place and function with relative ease, and above all where that understanding takes place in terms of a constantly smooth-running operation.

Institutions must have a bureaucracy to allow for clear definition of jobs. In homes for the aged and nursing homes these definitions are detailed, and they have a dramatic effect on life for residents. The definitions which tend to force a tight structuring of responsibility come from government, unions and home administrators.

Mr. Fletcher is a resident in an Ontario government-run home for the aged. He is 72 years old. He entered the home following a stroke and has difficulty with speech and the use of his left leg and arm. In all other respects he is a healthy, intelligent and articulate person. Mr. Fletcher entered the home for two reasons: he could no longer function in the community; he hoped for rehabilitation in the home. Mr. Fletcher was promised help on both counts.

Ontario's homes for the aged seem especially designed for people like Mr. Fletcher. As early as 1962 the Provincial Geriatric Study Centre provided an intensive short training programme for six specially chosen staff from homes for the aged. The programme was designed to give the six some insight into the problems of aging with particular reference to the "physical, emotional, and social difficulties of withdrawn non-communicative residents) . . ." The six, however, received more than insight; they were specifically *trained to help stroke victims* through basic exercises. The training course lasted only a few weeks. Soon the programme became "institutionalized." The number of specially trained persons increased from six in 1962 to 120 in 1974. A total of 87 homes run by government had one or more of the newly trained persons on their staff. Apparently, homes for the aged had increased their capacity to care for and assist in the rehabilitation of stroke victims such as Mr. Fletcher.

But a closer look reveals a different picture. The first six people trained as helpers held no professional degree; they were employees on the regular staff of a home for the aged who had worked there for more than six months, had some practical nursing skills, and, above all, had a caring feeling for the residents. The six were upgraded, and those who followed were similarly upgraded. The qualifications for training remained the same, except that they were formalized and made part of the job description.

The helpers are called "adjuvants." With the encouragement of government, the best of the general staff, who saw home residents in a variety of ways, were segregated. The adjuvant has become a specialist member of the "Care Team" and provides a specific service — exercise. The adjuvant must not be involved in the daily life of the home in any different capacity, otherwise it would be a "waste" of the money the government had spent on training.

The adjuvant, once a general senior employee, now fulfils, in the words of government, "a unique function in the Home." While connected with the functions of nursing and activities, the adjuvant is treated in a special manner. This means the adjuvant is responsible only to the administrator. Adjuvants shape their own world of forms and papers and reports. Where there are two or more adjuvants in a home, it is possible for one to receive the title Senior Adjuvant. And, for those who aspire to the rank, the administrator can call a person an Acting Adjuvant pending "certification," that is, completion of the one-month government training programme.

Mr. Fletcher, like every other resident, must adjust his life to fit institutional functions. A few times each week a porter will take him from his room to the adjuvant facility. There he will be treated and then released to another department staffed by another "specialist." In such a setting, how is it possible for Mr. Fletcher to feel "at home"? How is it possible for him to feel other than aliented? Why is this necessary? Couldn't the adjuvant's function be carried out by senior employees with generalized duties? What does tight job classification and specialization do except remove specialists from contact with the general life in the home?

Adjuvants are only one illustration of the pressure for specialization. They are awarded the right to remove themselves from contact with the general life of the home because they have stayed as employees for six months, are caring people and have had a month's training. Government leaves no doubt as to this:

> Because adjuvants are generally endowed with "take charge" capabilities they are often required to run bingos, dances and other general Home entertainment as well as to supervise residents' trips to clinics, shopping, etc. It would appear that this is a waste of adjuvant training. The adjuvant programme of classes and activities must receive first priority so that it can take place with reliable regularity if residents are to receive lasting benefits.

Employees like being adjuvants. They claim special categories — and higher pay scales. For they are no longer just senior employees, they are adjuvants, or they are nurses aides, or they are recreation directors. In a sense, this same specialization serves bureaucracy. The director of the home must lay down rules, such as those governing adjuvants, which define job functions. There is a need for such rules: adjuvants or nurses aides or recreation directors are trained to perform certain functions and therefore they must not step outside their boundaries. Similarly, none but those properly certified may perform the functions of the specialists. To do so would be a breach of professionalism. (It follows that someone must interpret and enforce the rules. This is the task of the administrator, a task which gives the administrator even greater power over the staff of the home.)

If specialization serves employees and administrators, does it also serve residents? After all, residents are the reason for the home's existence. Both government and the private sector can point to the rules and the specialists and recite functions that homes are performing which they never did before. Moreover, they can argue that these functions are being carried out by employees with a heightened sense of dedication. As professionals, they can state that residents who complain about the effects of professionalism really do not understand what is in their own best interests. But how does the system work? An outsider took her own view of that system.

A View from the Outside[4]

Fifteen-year-old Miriam Baum has a concern for the aged. With a social worker's assistance, she was chosen as a "volunteer" for a Toronto home. After an interview with the home's recreation director, she was formally accepted. (She was not introduced to nor did she meet the home administrator who stayed cloistered in her office.) Miriam kept a diary:

> For a home with about 100 residents there are two people in the activities department. This is hardly enough. (But the Administrator, so I was told, thinks not even two are needed.) One of the two is very experienced. The other one was only recently trained. They both came to the home only a short time ago. Before they came to the home there were almost no activities for the residents. Now there are many activities, and many more being planned. Now the residents have exercises (except on Saturday and Sunday when the staff are off duty), macramé, classes, games, outings, movies, pub nights, birthday parties, and singing sessions.
>
> Having these activities is still new to the people and so they are reluctant to try them. The residents on the lower floors (two and three, and a few on four) don't like to be associated with the more senile and ill residents on the upper floors (four, five and six). For outings the nurses decide who is healthy enough to participate. This means that those on the upper floors cannot go.
>
> The staff (not those in the office), that is, the nurses, caretakers, and people in activities seem to care a great deal about the residents. For most of the staff it is a very personal sort of job. Yet, on the sixth floor I have sometimes heard a nurse threaten or scream at a resident. But it doesn't happen too often.
>
> The activity room has been in operation for a year. The (supervisor of activities) told me that the home administrator has never been down to see what it's like. The (supervisor of activities) told me that everyone on salary has to be on guard because the administrator is constantly hassling everyone. . . .
>
> When I walked into the lobby of the home, it looked like it could almost be a hotel. There is carpeting, a beautiful dining room, a lounge, and even fancy lights. . . . The second floor has carpeting and a decent lounge area. It appears to be a sane place to stay. They even have pretty bed clothes. The third, fourth, fifth, and sixth floors go downhill in [ascending] order. On the third floor there is no carpeting and there is a smaller lounge area. There is also a faintly bad smell in the air. The fourth floor is the same.

The fifth and sixth floors have chairs attached to the walls all over the floor. That is their lounge. The air smells like a garbage dump. It's horribly loud with people everywhere. It seems to be overcrowded. I have heard that the home can't get enough staff for the sixth floor and I believe it. The sixth floor is where the so-called sick and senile residents are located. It seems that a lot of them just sit in their little chairs the entire day, talking to themselves. It's like they are animals in invisible cages.

When I came to the sixth floor for the first time, I was afraid of these people breaking out of their chains and leaping at me. The old men stared at me with empty eyes and hanging mouths, with their teeth clicking. When some of them started walking toward me, I couldn't be sure if they wanted to strangle me or pat my back and tell me I was a good girl. And there was an old lady who screamed at me when I bounced a ball to her husband too many times. [Miriam was sent to the sixth floor on her first day as a volunteer. Her duty was to bounce a small basketball to residents and have them bounce it back to her.] There are the majority of residents who fell asleep the moment I turned my back. Until I got used to this, I was afraid they would never wake up. I don't worry anymore about that. Finally, there are ladies who frown all day. But when I put my arms around them, they will smile. If I am lucky they will give me a kiss. . . . But I am constantly on guard because I don't know what to expect. . . .

No matter how much the home does for the residents, it can't take away the rejected feelings or disgusted thoughts of being placed in an institution. . . .

Miriam's diary is limited to one home. It is not openly critical, but factual: an administrator removed from life in the home; residents segregated; their frustration and fear. Yet what Miriam in her gentle way did not say an Ontario government study on long-term health care did declare in 1974. It set out the goals of the nursing home industry — as seen by government: "The nursing home is expected to provide . . . Activation and Remotivation programs; a stimulating social environment . . . [and] community interest and concern. . . ."

The 1974 study found "the areas where greatest deficiency has been recognized [in the nursing home industry] are in . . . failure to provide a stimulating social environment; failure to involve community interest in the homes; [and] failure to stimulate physician involvement in home standards. . . ." The study urged that homes be "educated to exploit the potential of the aging population by socially stimulating attitudes and programs." With such programmes would come positive benefits.

The study made this very pointed observation: *"It is a well recognized fact, that the more time placed in remotivation programs, the less staff time is required for nursing and personal care."*

In the nursing home where she served as a volunteer Miriam found "remotivation programs" rather far down on the administrator's priority list. What programming existed came without her support; in fact, the staff believed the administrator would cut that programme of activity if she could. The findings of the Ontario study of 1974 are precisely the same as Miriam's, except that they are more general.

The study indicated that there was no insurmountable difficulty in a home gearing up to "remotivation" of residents; in providing a stimulating social environment; and in involving the community. Remotivation has largely to do with attitudes. "Emphasis on training seminars for the [general] staff is one [approach]. [But such emphasis] must be ongoing as a means to utilize quiescent talents of residents of long-term care facilities." The feeling was that change could occur if only the home administration and the staff had the will. In itemized fashion the study dealt with corrective measures:

1. Stimulating social environment can be accomplished by:
   (a) Education of staff and administration.
   (b) Open door policy toward visitors and the community.
   (c) Staff assuming responsibility to work with volunteers.
   (d) Development of residents' councils with staff participation.
   (e) Greater use of newspapers and radio to maintain contact with and concern for the community.
   (f) Colour — brightness and light affect mood.
   (g) Reality orientation therapy programmes.
2. Community involvement is frequently a reflection of staff attitudes. These can be improved by:
   (a) Individuals contributing to conversations.
   (b) Groups in programmes and outings.
   (c) Unrestricted visiting hours.

What was said of nursing homes was repeated with some modification a year later in another provincial study. The question was put whether the *same* co-insurance rate should be charged in old age facilities when homes for the aged offer *varying* programme content and some nursing homes offer little, if any, programme content. The question might well indicate a reason for nursing homes' failure to remotivate and fully involve staff in a programme which might assist residents to integrate into the community and leave the home. Nursing homes and homes for the aged are not paid for the people they return to society. Rather, they are paid in accordance with the number who remain marginally incapacitated, and removed from the community.

CHAPTER FIVE

Law: Words Alone?

Government stands frustrated because it lacks effective sanctions to order change.

A Cruel Hoax: The Quebec Experience[1]

It was with pride that in 1974, Louis Novick, executive director of Maimonides Hospital and Home for the Aged of Montreal, described to an audience of professionals involved with care of the elderly the sweeping new legislation of Quebec. The Quebec government was going to regulate every form of care for the aged. The law would protect the elderly by allowing them full care in the context of individual freedom. The more than 185,000 persons over 65 living in Montreal, for example, would have local home care opportunities. And if they were in need of an institutional setting in which to live, they would find programmes there to enhance the quality of life and also be able to share in the control of the home. The entire programme was to be administered by a single government agency, not divided between a number of agencies as in Ontario. Within each Quebec institution serving the long-term elderly resident, Mr. Novick said, the government was determined to ensure an environment conducive to the development of each person's abilities.

The government phrase is *humanisation des soins* ("humanizing of care"). The law requires that every hospital centre for long-term patients and every home care centre must have a committee of patients elected by all the others. Called the "recipient's committee," the elected group in law has power of liaison between the patients and the institution's board of directors and executive director. The committee is charged with protecting the general interests of the patients by forwarding recommendations to the institution's directors and by helping to organize leisure programmes for the patients.

The right, indeed the duty, of residents' participation in the control of the institution does not end with the committee of recipients. Every chronic care hospital and every home care centre for adults (the equivalent of a nursing home) is required to have its patients or residents elect two of their number to serve on the institution's board of directors:

Moreover, in conjunction with the Quebec Department of Education, an in-service training program, for non-professional staff, particularly nursing aides and orderlies, has been established to ensure a better understanding on the part of the staff of the needs of long-term patients and how to satisfy them. . . . The Chaplain, be he minister, rabbi, or priest, has been recognized by the Department of Social Affairs as a full-fledged professional on the staff of the long-term institution whose salary is to be included within the global budget for which the Department assumes responsibility.

Central to the new regulatory scheme is the tight control of homes run for profit. The government decided to make human need, not money the primary reason for operating nursing homes. Only those which had been established under the law — which were termed "public establishments" — or non-profit corporations could continue. Private nursing homes with more than twenty beds were prohibited. Moreover, the control of the small homes had to be cooperative, that is, residents would participate significantly in the home's operations. All other homes for the aged would be either under the ownership of government or charitable organizations.

Quebec law eliminated the profit motive and substituted instead a regulatory scheme that centred on the care of the individual. Mr. Novick had spoken of admission procedures at Maimonides: "We have found in our experience that in order to determine whether an individual is legitimately in need of long-term care, it is necessary to have some medical information sent by the doctor, but also nursing evaluation, and social service evaluation. Even the medical information sent by the outside doctor has to be scrutinized by a doctor connected with the long-term facility as to its validity." At Maimonides, nurses even make home visits to applicants. The institution could gear itself quite easily to the new regulatory scheme of government. It would screen applicants for admission, and assist those rejected to find other day care facilities. Maimonides could allow those admitted participation within the meaning of the law. To Maimonides and other well-run institutions in Quebec the new law was quite acceptable. To some extent it codified existing practice and seemed to ease pressure for admission by promising a developed community structure to assist older people.

However, for many the new law was a cruel hoax. Certainly, it established a structure concerning the care of the aged. But care does not come from words alone. The statute book is not the same as available beds or properly run day care facilities. In the Montreal area alone there is an estimated shortage of more than two thousand beds with people on waiting lists for more than two years.

Two years after the new law was enacted the *Montreal Star* estimated 323 unlicensed (underground) nursing homes were operating in the province. They exist for those who are not able to obtain accommodation in the licensed homes and are unable to afford decent private care. This does not mean, however, that the law is a dead letter. It did have one result: it drove privately run nursing homes either out of business or underground) The government could point to its legislation and some examples of successful application of the law, such as Maimonides. And the government could leave undisturbed a festering sore — the underground nursing homes.

What is government to do? If a home is closed where are the residents to go? Existing licensed facilities are already full. Government, it can be said, is tolerating a known condition. It is as if an unholy alliance has been entered upon between government and some elements of the business community to allow, even encourage, the very principle the law was designed to eliminate: nursing homes should not be run for profit.)

It would not be difficult for the government of Quebec to put the underground nursing homes out of business. The government does not have to rely upon licence powers or heavy penalties. It need only make the budgetary commitment to cause the paper promises to come alive. Once good homes are established at little or no cost to their residents, the profiteering homes would cease operations. No one would pay more money for inferior care. Apparently, it is not in the interest of the government of Quebec to give reality to its paper policies. The *Montreal Star*, in a series of three articles by Don Braid, probed the underground homes. They do not have to solicit business; relatives and older people search for them. The cost of "care" could be as little as $130 a month, a person's entire pension. These are homes outside the law; there is no need for the owners, in business for profit, to be overly sensitive to patients' needs. As a result, the conditions that prevail in the underground homes, which are nearly always full, often tend to lack humanity and even to be unsafe.

The *Montreal Star* probe made these findings in its survey: ∕

— Often there was no dining room or common room. Residents were confined to their beds for the entire day.
— Nutrition frequently was poor. The probe discovered homes where residents' meals consisted only of soup and Jello. Hospitals

reported receiving patients from underground homes who were
suffering from malnutrition.
— Care was limited. In one home a single person cared for nineteen
elderly people. In another home residents were fed dinner at 4:30
P.M. after which they were put in their rooms to sleep. This was
done to relieve the staff of further care.
— Physical abuse was not unknown. One resident was thrown to the
floor twice as punishment for attempting to use the telephone after
4 P.M. in violation of the home rule.

This list is not exhaustive; the horror stories seem to have no end. The
real question is why they have to occur. The lesson of Quebec is the
realization that legal reforms alone will not correct abuses. Even
enforcement of the law through rigorous inspection will not do so. The
Montreal Star wrote of a home which had been closed on four different
occasions yet continued to operate. It continued to operate because it
was profitable. Such homes fill a need, and government has not yet
filled the vacuum by constructing quality nursing homes and day care
centres.

A Different Path: The Ontario Experience[2]

Ontario followed a path different from Quebec's. In 1972, as a
preliminary to passing the Nursing Home Act, the government of
Ontario surveyed its private nursing home industry in order to formulate
a policy that would ensure a minimum level of care. Of 483 nursing
homes operating in Ontario about half had fewer than 50 residents. The
smaller nursing homes frequently were owned and operated by a single
person (such as a widowed nurse.) And that owner and operator
constituted the professional staff. The rates in the smaller homes ranged
from $10 to $15 a day. There were also large and luxurious homes
where owners had spent up to $13,000 per bed, were paying 14 per cent
interest on second mortgages, and expected to recover their capital
investment by charging residents as much as $25 a day.

The unregulated system simply did not serve those most in need of
nursing care. Many residents, particularly those in the smaller homes,
were retired. They had chosen to live there more for the convenience
than any real medical need. They wanted ''custodial'' care: housekeeping services such as cooking, laundry and cleaning.

At the same time, there were those in need of skilled nursing care
who were living alone in boarding houses, in overcrowded homes for

the aged (sometimes with as many as twelve to a room) or with families who could not afford the cost of nursing home care. And of those families that turned to nursing homes, all but the most affluent were strained financially by the expense. It was the severity of this financial burden as well as a desire to provide nursing home care wherever medically necessary that finally prompted the Ontario government to act in 1972.

The legislation had two prongs. First, (it entitled anyone requiring extended care to be covered by the Ontario Health Insurance Plan.) And secondly, it provided in considerable detail, standards by which licensed nursing homes were to be operated.) (It was unlawful to administer nursing care to two or more unrelated persons *without* a licence.) These standards were embodied in regulations dealing with the physical (structure of the home, fire protection, personnel and, most important, the rates a home could charge and the percentage of its beds that were to be set aside for ward accommodations, that is, four persons to a room. (Because private and semi-private accommodations were generally more profitable, many owners had a disproportionately small number of ward rooms. The regulations, of course, also had the general effect of prohibiting owners from assigning *more* than four persons to a room.)

As of April 1, 1972, in order to maintain its licence a nursing home had to provide 75 per cent of its residents with extended care. Anything less was considered "custodial" or "intermediate" care, for which the resident had to pay the entire cost. Furthermore, 60 per cent of a nursing home's accommodation was to be available at ward rates which the government then set at $12.50 a day, irrespective of what residents had paid for comparable accommodations in the past. (Of that $12.50, $9.00 was to be paid by the government, and $3.50 by the resident.)

There was anxious speculation throughout the nursing home industry about the effect of the new law. It was clear enough that the act aimed at large-scale, professionally managed homes and that many of the smaller homes would simply be out of business if the majority of their residents were paying only $12.50 per day. More precisely, it was estimated that it would require approximately fifty residents to survive economically. (In 1976 unofficial estimates cited sixty as the minimum number.)

The Ministry of Health foresaw this as a probable outcome but hoped that many of the small homes would continue as retirement homes. Since these homes in many cases already had a high proportion of persons requiring only custodial care, the government hoped that such a transition would be feasible. (Further, according to government, the 75 per cent quota for extended care would gradually be increased so that ultimately all nursing home beds would be occupied by residents who actually required medical attention.)

Owners attacked the government's reimbursement scheme for its inflexibility. They claimed that a flat-rate system failed to take into account the higher costs homes incurred in caring for some kinds of patients (for example, terminal cancer patients). In place of the proposed plan they favoured a system directly related to their costs. (American nursing homes also are usually reimbursed on a cost-plus basis, that is, their costs plus a reasonable profit.) This criticism was restated a year later by an arbitration board in its award to a bargaining unit of non-professional nursing home employees. After noting that hospitals receive comparable increases in their operating budgets after arbitration awards, it stated: "It would appear the method of reimbursement bears little if any relationship to actual capital and operating costs. It is readily evident that under these conditions nursing home employers may well become the victims of a fixed income-variable squeeze."

The government, while agreeing in principle that a more equitable system might eventually be developed, was unprepared at the time to make any costly changes until more was known about the new programme. (As it was, the $31 million initially budgeted for the programme proved to be grossly inadequate.)

Before April 1972 newspaper articles reported that a large number of homes would defy the Nursing Home Act and refuse to admit as residents applicants insured by OHIP to pay only the minimum daily rate. Dissident owners held meetings and presented a counter-proposal to the government that the per diem rate be raised to $14.50. Despite the threats and the controversy, when the act actually went into effect no real opposition materialized. Government had repeatedly warned that any homes failing to admit OHIP patients would no longer be licensed, and as there was still a considerable demand for licences from prospective owners willing to comply with the legislation no effective resistance was possible. In fact, one owner in Scarborough operating a three-hundred-bed home claimed he had been making a profit by charging only $11 a day and considered the passage of the Nursing Home Act a windfall. At the programme's beginning, 448 of the province's homes agreed to participate while only two decided that they would not and, as a result, operated as retirement homes rather than licensed nursing homes.

Many of the licensed homes faced serious problems to comply with the regulations governing the physical structure of the nursing home, which specified the size of bedrooms and dining rooms, the widths of corridors, the heights of windows, and the number of fire escapes a home was to have. Government provisions, in effect, were a mandate to nursing homes to standardize. Where a building had not originally been designed as a nursing home but had been adapted, compliance was particularly difficult. Homes were ordered to resemble "posh motels," said one owner. He was faced with $125,000 in renovation expenses in order to provide the requisite ninety square feet per person in a home that had been converted from an old shoe factory, even though the residents apparently were entirely contented with the existing conditions.

Another owner who had won a number of awards for the quality of his facility discovered it was now substandard because his dining room, lounges and activity areas were not large enough, and he had two colour and two black and white television sets instead of four radios. Compliance became extremely expensive considering that extended care coverage was also being offered by municipal and charitable homes which were not paying the same high interest rates on mortgages nor being subjected to the same taxes.

At the same time, there were those who maintained that residents should have the right voluntarily to enter homes that provided *better* services than those government compelled, but at a higher price. The owner of Country Place in Richmond Hill, for example, in 1972 was operating a de luxe home in which all of the residents received at least 2½ hours of care a day. Furthermore, the building was only a single storey high (thus greatly facilitating exit in case of fire), air-conditioned, fitted with glare-free windows, and had special chairs, from which the residents could more easily get up. Under the new scheme those desiring additional conveniences would, like everyone else, be forced to apply to homes whose overall design and policies were largely determined by the fact that the preponderance of beds were generating an income of only $12.50 a day.

Further problems arose over the new legislation's eligibility provisions. While the ministry originally had established the "1½ hours of nursing care" standard and estimated that it would cover between 75 to 80 per cent of those living in nursing homes at that time, doubts remained as to how the standard was to be applied in individual cases.

Less than a month after the programme began, 8,000 were denied coverage while 23,000 had qualified. Controversy arose when many who needed a great deal of attention, but not actual nursing care, were ruled ineligible. A 103-year-old woman was rejected, for example, because the only medical assistance she required was administering her daily insulin shots. Another woman, 91 years old, who was taking heart medicine and too senile to care for herself, was also turned down because most of the care she received was considered non-nursing, and therefore outside the scope of the statute. In general, senility was not an insured disability due to a confusing distinction drawn between physical and psychological infirmities. And, finally, many felt that qualified people were being excluded because too much discretion was left to private physicians, who in many cases saw their elderly patients only infrequently and were unfamiliar with the forms upon which placement decisions were based.

In spite of all the difficulties, however, by August of 1972, 32,000 persons had been approved for OHIP nursing home coverage out of the 48,000 who had applied. At the time applications were averaging 150 per day from people either in private residences or in hospitals. Serious shortages were developing, and long waiting lists existed for many homes, particularly those that formerly had been charging premium rates. This heightened demand coupled with the narrow profit margin led homes to scrutinize carefully those seeking admittance. Anyone needing only the minimum of care was generally preferred over those demanding more attention.

The situation was aggravated when many of the smaller homes were driven out of business. In the first five months twenty homes were forced to close and sixteen more were put up for sale. (Over sixty more closed in the following year). Perhaps the most serious consequence of this upheaval was that thousands of residents were displaced because they required either too little or too much care to remain in a nursing home.

On the other hand, despite the trauma of moves from one institution to another, and despite the waiting lists to enter nursing homes or homes for the aged, the province of Ontario has not had the scourge of underground nursing homes. Ontario acted to regulate the nursing home industry; to control and not eliminate the private sector, while at the same time increasing the number of government-run homes for the aged. Within a range, Ontario brought all nursing homes to the same level of care, and a kind of homogenized institution was established in law and in practice. Government inspectors could go from one home to another and find little difference — if government regulations were, in fact, followed: the same rooms; the same service; the same food and the same recreational facilities. The expectations of government could be summarized by the promise of a well-known motel chain: there are no surprises at a Holiday Inn.

The government of Ontario did not impose an ideal state. It could only be called a livable state. Sameness often brings with it a certain monotonous quality. Major innovations are discouraged because they interfere with uniform regulations. People and functions tend to be categorized and specialized. But the Ontario kind of regulation has had its benefits: at a marginal level the basic physical needs of the elderly have been met.

Inspection: A Study of Limitations[3]

With regard to compliance with Ontario nursing home regulations, where the industry is more highly regulated than most other provinces (or, for that matter, in the United States), there are no independent means of evaluation. And the government makes no attempts to explain the state of the industry, so that the public can determine just how well its policy is working. But this much is known of the quality of government inspection in Ontario: (there is a highly trained staff to do the job; the instructions to the staff are detailed, and their access to nursing homes unlimited.) Moreover, they will investigate and report every complaint relating to a nursing home.

The inspection staff is divided into Divisions of Nursing, Environment and Fire. For inspection purposes, the province is split into three geographical areas. Each area has inspectors regularly assigned from each division to ensure familiarity and continual communication with each licensed nursing home. It is a matter of some pride to the Inspection Branch that whatever local standards may be, such as municipal fire ordinances, it imposes its own higher standards.

Inspectors know all too well that homes may be made to look nice in anticipation of official visits.) The Nursing Division states that it makes at least one unannounced visit to each home every three months and one annual complete licensing inspection. The Environmental and Fire Divisions also conduct a complete inspection of each licensed home annually.

At one point inspectors, in the view of senior supervisors, were unduly "rigid" in their approach. Residents were examined by nursing inspectors as if "they were under a microscope." Those who were confined to bed were undressed and subjected to a physical examination for bed sores. (Ontario regulations require that bedridden residents be turned over every hour.) Other residents were examined to determine if finger and toe nails were cut and if they had been bathed with regularity. Some home administrators and residents felt this was an invasion of privacy. They pressed for and obtained a more subtle and tactful kind of inspection.

An inspector's job can best be done (by using objective tests). If regulations, such as turning residents in bed, are specific, they can be enforced. An inspector knows what to look for and how to draft an efficient report. If regulations are vague, they cannot be enforced. Yet objective tests alone can further a resident's sense of alienation, of being treated as a thing whose condition is examined to see whether it is in good working order. The regulations in Saskatchewan, certainly one of the more progressive provinces, highlight the difficulty in framing useful criteria in proof of a standard of adequate care. The regulations demand that guests (residents) shall "at all times show evidence of adequate care."

— Criteria for determining adequate care shall include appearance of good personal hygiene, such as clean, healthy appearing skin, clean trimmed fingernails and toe nails, clean and neatly groomed hair, clean teeth and mouth, and an absence of cracked lips;
— evidence of an attempt to create as cheerful and home-like [an] environment as possible;
— evidence that guests are encouraged to be up and dressed in their own personal clothing for at least a brief period every day, unless ordered otherwise by a doctor. . . .

The Saskatchewan standards are clear. That is, a home administrator can understand what the government expects. To enforce those standards, as a matter of law, is another matter. Inspectors can physically examine guests for clean teeth and mouths or an absence of cracked lips. But what is an inspector to say of an administrator's attempt to "create as cheerful and home-like an environment as possible?" It is a risky business for an inspector to criticize a home as "drab." Isn't that a matter of personal taste? Isn't the inspector to be an impartial fact-finder? A difference remains between what the law can expect and what it can enforce.

Still, Ontario has apparently overcome what might have been the primary cause in the United States for massive nursing home violations. There, government has poured enormous sums into a highly regulated industry. In 1970, consumer advocate Ralph Nader wrote:

The full scope of nursing home abuses and profiteering has yet to be told. Although the Federal government pours over a billion dollars a year into this two-and-a-half billion dollar industry through Medicare and other subsidy programs, there have never been full-fledged Congressional hearings, nor the enforcement of adequate Federal and state standards, nor the administrative inquiries and disclosures that are needed to reduce the institutional violence and cruelty that are rampant. Such moves have not occurred in spite of major fire disasters, fatal food contaminations, corporate manipulations, drug experimentation beyond proper medical discretion, kickbacks in drug sales to residents, abysmal lack of medical supervision, and strong evidence that such abuses are more epidemic than episodic.

(Not long after Nader wrote this, Congress did initiate a sweeping investigation of the nursing home industry.)

In the United States, the federal government assigned the enforcement of stringent regulations to the states, and from the states to county and local boards of health or other officials. There was no unified, well-trained and disciplined inspection system as in Ontario. Moreover, the number of homes and their scattering throughout the United States only increased the problems coming from a fragmented and generally poorly trained inspection staff. (Ontario purposely cut the number of nursing homes ensuring, on the whole, that the fewer and necessarily larger homes would be able to turn a reasonable profit. It is fair to say that the state of the nursing home industry in Ontario is radically different from that in the United States. This is the result of effective regulation and reasonable financing.

It is also fair to say that Ontario is not without its problems. Not long after the 1972 regulations came into force in Ontario, government felt impelled to launch a series of criminal complaints against some nursing homes. Informally, though it was known in the industry, government was aware of "broad and glaring infractions of regulations." In the view of government the criminal complaints were successful. They resulted in fines of about $1,000 each against three nursing homes.

Although it is true that every Ontario complaint is investigated, in nursing homes these complaints are not likely to come from residents. Indeed, it will take a persistent relative or friend to find out where to file a complaint. There is no government inspector on the premises ready to receive and act upon a grievance. There is no grievance mechanism. There is no smooth, well-known means for grievances to be passed directly from the complainant to the government for action. Residents are not afforded any statement of rights when they enter nursing homes. They do not know what in law they might claim as theirs. And, if they were ever told of their rights, they would not know where to turn for enforcement. Even if they did know what agency to telephone, only the most courageous of them would do so. There is no protection in law against an administrator's anger or reprisals.

In this respect government-run homes for the aged are quite different from nursing homes. The law does require such homes to establish a grievance mechanism for residents. More to the point, no resident will be punished for using the grievance machinery. Ontario statutes provide that *every* home administrator shall "establish and follow a regular procedure for the hearing of *any* grievance of *any* resident of the home, correct the grievance if he considers it necessary and maintain a written record of all such hearings."

How different nursing homes are from the working world. Any employer who has recognized a union and entered into a collective agreement knows that all employees, as of right, have a means of redress. The agreement sets out the terms and conditions of employment between the employer and, through the union, the employees. The employees know their rights and their responsibilities. They have approved the agreement and carry copies of it in their pockets.

If an employee believes he has been unjustly treated under the agreement, he has an absolute right to call upon the grievance machinery. The employee has the right to approach the union, and the union has the right to approach management concerning the dispute. If the question cannot be resolved, and if the union cares to press the matter, it can demand arbitration, a hearing and a decision before an impartial chairperson binding upon the parties. All this is possible without the employee feeling there is any danger to the job or the potential for advancement.

The procedure available to unions and managements, required by legislation, is largely unheard of in nursing homes. Indeed, in confidential talks with Ontario inspectors the point was made that residents are seldom interviewed concerning any complaint. "The residents are not free to talk to us." They are too frightened to do so.

Actual mistreatment, actual malnutrition are the exception rather than the rule in Ontario homes but they do happen. The wrongdoers are known to government. And, more often than not, government, because it lacks effective sanctions to compel changes, stands frustrated over a period of months and sometimes years before the wrongs are corrected.

It is no easy matter to document mistreatment of residents in nursing homes or homes for the aged. There are no published studies by government Inspection Branch officials which provide an overview of compliance with regulations by nursing homes and homes for the aged. Those matters which government bring to hearing either before the regulatory agency or the courts are relatively few. Moreover, government will bring issues to hearing only when all other efforts at settlement have failed. Between 1972 and 1976 a total of eleven complaints was filed by government against nursing homes in Ontario that could have led to loss of licences or fines. The hearings themselves are matters of public record — at least that is what the law declares. In fact, the hearings are not widely reported by the media, and attempts to find and study the records are frustrated by government.

In August 1973, an 87-year-old woman fell to her death from a home fire escape. On seven different occasions an inspector had reported a faulty alarm system on the door leading to the fire escape. The same report had been made by the local fire department inspector. Yet the home had taken no action. Nor had the government imposed sanctions to enforce its finding of violation. In June 1974, another Ontario nursing home pleaded guilty to five offences and was fined a total of $1,000. The offences related to personnel requirements: there was neither a registered nurse nor a registered nursing assistant on duty at night. An unauthorized member of the staff administered drugs. In entering a guilty plea the home owner explained that no harm was intended. But what could be done? The violations were a direct result of employment problems. There was then a scarcity of registered nurses and registered nursing assistants. The home owner estimated that about half of the provincial homes were similarly understaffed. (One month later still another home was fined $1,000 for similar violations of personnel requirements.) Other examples are on record.

The central facts are these: (1) No one, not even government, fully understands the quality of a home's compliance with law, because the source for complaints, the residents themselves, is not protected and encouraged to speak. (2) Even when violations of a most flagrant kind are found, the enforcement branch of government can do little.

On March 8, 1976, the Ottawa *Journal* surveyed some Ottawa nursing homes. The investigation disclosed "that not all nursing staffs lack empathy nor do all abuse their patients. . . . Unfortunately, the visits also turned up some appalling nursing home conditions, which, when brought to the attention of the ministry of health in Toronto received rapid investigation.'' Note that the *Journal* did *not* write that the complaints resulted in rapid corrective action.

The *Journal* described a specific home where its staff conducted a ''tour'' that ''revealed an atmosphere of hopelessness, barren rooms, patients with vacant faces, personal grooming that left something to be desired, and an administrative staff constantly besieged by problems and staff worries. . . . Patients crowded into the main 'lobby' of the converted hotel and sat on broken-down couches or kitchen-style chairs. There was no music, no bright lighting, no living plants, no conversation, no television. Just the cold draft of air which swept through the corridors every time the outside door opened onto the chill February morning.''

What the Ottawa *Journal* reported on March 8 had been observed and noted by an inspector two months earlier. The inspector visited the home as a result of ''numerous complaints.'' As a direct result of the inspector's statement, the home was ''ordered'' to initiate a programme of improvements in accordance with specifications laid out by the regulatory authority. The home's plans for adopting the programme were to be presented to government by January 30. By March 8 the home had yet to respond, to make *any* contact with government. Indeed, the owner of the home, a physician, told the Ottawa *Journal* he had not even heard of the government complaints: ''Nobody has approached me about this . . . I just can't believe there is anything wrong.'' Months later some corrective action was taken. Eventually the home was sold.

A spokesperson for the regulatory authority explained why government could not do more except continually inspect, persuade and ultimately impose sanctions such as fines: ''Let me stress that we are not anxious to close any nursing home because the need for such institutions is great. We would prefer to develop an atmosphere of cooperation which would be of mutual benefit.'' Indeed, government went out of its way to assure the one hundred residents of the home, their relatives and friends that the home would not be closed. To do so would be to punish the residents further. In order to remedy a condition of inhumanity is government to put the residents on the street, to deny them lodging, to take them away from the only community they know?

In the context of existing law the dilemma of government is insuperable The ultimate weapon of government, to close the home, is too powerful; it would destroy the very people the law is intended to protect.

Laws, however, can be reformed. New approaches could obviate the dilemma. In Ontario, it is the owner of the home who is licensed. Little is said about the operating head of the home, the administrator, other than that such a person is "responsible for [the home] administration and shall be deemed to be an employee."(Anyone wishing to become an administrator must be eighteen; free of any communicable disease; willing to undergo mental and physical tests of fitness to work in a home; hold a high school diploma or have "satisfactory" work experience. Absolutely nothing is said about licensing the administrator, nor about an owner empowering an administrator to comply with government rules as a condition of ownership.

What Ontario requires of a nursing home administrator stands in sharp contrast to what the province imposes upon an administrator of a government-run home. Such an administrator must have completed a course of instruction approved by government. In addition, the administrator must "have a specialized knowledge of and adequate experience in modern methods of administering a home; have a sympathetic understanding of problems pertaining to the needs of elderly persons residing in a home and a suitable personality for the position; and have the ability to retain the confidence of the staff and direct it efficiently." Having laid down these criteria, the regulations then vest the administrator with operating control over the home.

If the home described by the Ottawa *Journal* had had a licensed administrator, it is questionable whether the wrongs found would have been as aggravated. It is also questionable whether there would have been the same delay in responding to government orders. One may well ask whether older people paying for either all or a portion of their own care are not entitled to the same level of protection as those living in government-run homes.

CHAPTER SIX

A Matter of Dollars: Shaping Public Policy

"Despite the established trend away from institutional care, Ontario gives its seniors a strong financial incentive to go inside, especially those on Extended Care. . . . The irony is that very few people go inside institutions without a great deal of reluctance."
Ontario Government Report 1975

Streaming The Aged: From Hospitals to "Homes"[1]

Although the needs of the aged are a top priority for the government of Ontario the hard fact is that its central concern is to save money. A cutback in spending was essential, and new alternatives to institutionalization would have to be found.

This is not to deny Ontario's concern for the aged. The province provides more generous allowances than the others or, for that matter, most countries in the world. Ontario not only defines extended care very liberally, but allows individual doctors and nursing homes to determine residents' eligibility for that amenity. Some provinces, such as the Maritimes, because of more limited finances define extended care — as we shall see — in extremely narrow terms. Moreover, Ontario offers a guaranteed annual income (about $279 a month in 1977) for those over 65 which is exceeded only by Alberta (about $285 a month).

Judged by the standard of need, however, Ontario is not overly generous in the treatment of its senior citizens. Generally, they require, not major treatment, but a combination of checkups and care for the aches and minor troubles that come with bodies that have grown old. For these, they do not always need the care of physicians, but rather of paramedical people. The facts are beyond question. From 1969-1970 information, Ontario offered no orthoptic (eye) treatment unless performed by an opthalmologist, a highly specialized, highly priced, very busy medical doctor. British Columbia is more generous. It allows treatment, if authorized by a physician, up to *$25 a year*. The remaining provinces allow nothing.

Ontario ranks with the other provinces, except for British Columbia, by denying any compensation for physiotherapy — unless performed by physicians, with their equipment, at their offices. British Columbia allows $50 a year for such treatment — if ordered by a physician.

For chiropractic and osteopathic services Ontario has eased its position ever so slightly. On balance, it is alongside Alberta, British Columbia and Manitoba by permitting expenditures up to $100 per year. The remaining provinces allow nothing. For podiatric or chiropodic (foot) care Ontario again is in the lead by granting $100 a year. British Columbia allows up to $50 per year for each patient unless referred by a physician. Alberta agreed to $100 per patient, and $150 for each family. The other provinces offer nothing for such care.

In 1972, however, the chief concern of the Ontario government was the high cost of hospitalization. It was saddled not only with a large percentage of the cost of constructing more hospitals, but also with huge per diem patient costs. In Ontario the per diem costs in chronic care hospitals (where the aged were sent in increasingly large numbers) was $26.70 in 1970, and $36.70 in 1974. If elderly patients went to nursing homes or homes for the aged, government could cut the cost of patient care in half. Comparable costs in nursing homes were $12.50 for 1972, and $17 in 1974. Further, by removing chronic care patients from hospitals, government could make new beds available without the burden of building new hospitals.

Government achieved the goals set in 1972 by legislation that enabled it to take the necessary steps: a given percentage of bed space in nursing homes for extended care patients; a fixed rate of compensation for extended care; a limited charge beyond extended care for each person; and the means (welfare) for all individuals qualifying as extended care patients to receive nursing home care. About 90 per cent of the beds in Ontario nursing homes qualify for extended care payments. (Much of what has been said of nursing homes applies to government-run homes for the aged.) Government possesses power and suasion and has used them with notable effect.

Some telling figures also indicate the success of the Ontario government's fiscal programme: in 1970 there were 3,220 hospital beds for the chronic sick in the province; *in 1974 that figure remained unchanged*. In 1970 there were 500 private chronic care hospital beds. In 1974 that figure had *decreased* to 430 beds. In 1972 there were 19,132 nursing home beds. Two years later, despite the number of small nursing home closures, there were 22,875 nursing home beds, the overwhelming percentage of which qualified for extended care.

To maintain about 3,700 chronic care hospital beds for the chronic sick, the 1974-75 budget called for an expenditure of $85.5 million. To maintain 26,300 beds in government-run homes for the aged in the same year government budgeted $67.4 million. That is, government maintained more than seven times the number of patients in homes for the aged compared to chronic care facilities, at a cost that was more than $18 million cheaper. It made economic sense to limit the development of chronic care facilities and encourage the growth of homes for the aged and nursing homes.

Surely there is nothing wrong with government effecting savings in important social programmes if, at the same time, the goals of those programmes are achieved. But is government directing its efforts toward the rehabilitation of the aged, toward the fulfilment of life, or is it attempting to find an inexpensive and fairly humane way to warehouse the aged until they die? Certainly, government support as it exists is not directed toward maximizing life as much as it is geared toward relieving the financial pressure on hospital costs.

For instance, there is absolutely no assurance that Ontario's extended care programme is permanent. And it is this scheme that is the primary means for keeping patients in nursing homes. The costs of that programme have already become unbearable to the Ontario government.

Government already has the means to alter radically the extended care programme, which it can either eliminate or curtail as an insured service. To do so requires no act of the legislature, only, at most, regulations approved by the cabinet. "Administrative interpretation" would also achieve the same tightening of coverage. Presently, Ontario regulations are somewhat flexible in allowing physicians to certify an individual as in need of extended care. As a matter of interpretation, and without the need even for new regulations, government can make it far more difficult for an individual *to qualify* for extended care payments. Without such coverage each person would have to bear the *full cost* of custodial care under rates set by the government. In 1977, extended care payments, funded by government, amount to about $13 daily for each recipient, The added cost which the individual must bear is only about $6 daily. Residents in nursing homes, who are not receiving extended care, must find a way to pay the full $19 daily from their own pockets, since government will provide compensation only under the general welfare laws. That is, if the individual is indigent, government *might* be of assistance. Again, however, government controls the administration of welfare, and could easily provide housing assistance in the form of a subsidy, instead of paying the full cost of residential care in a nursing home or home for the aged.

There are signs that the administrative screws are being tightened; (eligibility for extended care in nursing homes and homes is about to be limited) In 1974, only two years after Ontario established its programme of extended care, came a report from the Interministerial Task Force on Long Term Care, which dealt with the obvious pressures resulting from the programme: nursing homes preferred(patients who marginally qualified for extended care;) as institutions concerned about costs, they wanted residents who needed only a minimum of nursing care, and still qualified for extended care payments. (They were (and are) selective in their admission policy) The Task Force recommended that decisions on applications for individual admissions be taken away from the institution and placed in an "area co-ordinating unit":

> All were acutely aware of the policies of some nursing homes in their selective admissions which has created difficulties in some areas of the province for admissions of persons whose total care needs could well be met in a nursing home, but that they would indeed require 3 or even 4 hours of skilled nursing and personal care, the great amount being personal care.
> The committee were in agreement that the home should not be the authority to assess needs as to suitability for admission if the homes are to be accepted as a part of the total health care system. It is accepted that with the establishment of an area co-ordinating unit, residents will have a comprehensive assessment and the most suitable service or facility determined by the Discharge Planning Hospital personnel, in conjunction with an assessment counsellor of the Co-ordinating unit.

Physicians responding to the financial needs of patients and their families exert another pressure for extended care. In 1975 came still another Interministerial Task Force report which was kept secret for two years. It referred to increased distortions in applications for extended care:

> As greater pressures were brought to bear on physicians to reduce personal costs of residents in Homes for the Aged and Nursing Homes, it seemed likely that more patients would be qualified for Extended Care whose needs might have been served at a less intensive level of care. Hand in hand with classification (as to the need for extended care) the need was seen(for admission control) Almost all of the facilities determined their own admission policies and practices without co-ordination or direction, and this appeared to result in substantial waste and inappropriate use of resources.

Re-Evaluation: Cutting Back[2]

Confused standards compounded the government's difficult financial situation. While (extended care was originally considered "another link" in a total health care package it was also an important means of relieving government of the heavy cost of chronic care hospitalization. Yet extended care in operation is geared more toward persons who need only marginal nursing care. With(occupancy rates of nearly 100 per cent, there is no financial incentive for nursing homes (or homes for the aged) to accept those in need of greater nursing care. *Even with a steady growth in the number of extended care beds, the basic facts have not changed:(more people are being qualified for extended care who need only marginal nursing help; more people in need of heavy nursing care are finding it increasingly difficult to find nursing home beds.)* So, far from saving money,(government found itself saddled with a programme that was institutionalizing more and more people.

In a 1975 memorandum, a government Task Force group saw little reason for expanding institutionalization; what it did see was a distinct group of about 55,000 adults, aged and ill, representing a highly unified aggregate of needs and served by similar facilities.

The Task Force report stated:

> It should be possible to develop a clear continuum of care (for the elderly) with defined levels of service, each level being accorded a specific cost. This would eliminate the artificial distinctions implied in the artificial labels, Nursing Home, Home for the Aged, Chronic Care, etc. It should be possible to control admission and flow to make the most of the beds available in contrast with the wasteful competition that now exists. Accusations and counter accusations are made between the facilities as they jockey for the best "mix" of clients. Since each facility determines its own admission policy and decides when to release a client, institutional gamesmanship detracts from service effectiveness. This effect is heightened when the competition is between profit oriented facilities and charitable and community facilities. . . .
>
> With varieties of legislation, standards, methods of supervision and inspection, funding and cost control spawn numerous offices and centres of authority in Government. [The institutionalized aged are] highly unified in needs and service modes. [Yet this group] is represented by more than twenty-four centres of authority in two Ministries, each Ministry having a basically different service philosophy.
>
> Standards, supervision, and funding follow the same highly varied patterns, confusing both to program personnel and public

alike. Perhaps the most serious matter is the lack of non-residential alternatives. Despite the established trend away from institutional care, Ontario gives its seniors a strong financial incentive to go inside, especially those on Extended Care. Firstly, they are able to live in a style they would be unable to pay for in the community out of OAS-GIS, GAINS, Family Benefits and pensions. Secondly, many of them can save money while in residence. In Toronto alone funds held in trust for residents of homes for the aged in Extended Care, saved out of the comfort allowance alone [pocket money given residents by the government], are estimated to be growing at over $1 million a year. On the death of the resident, these funds pass to the estate of the deceased. In the meantime the aged person in the community can barely make ends meet and has extremely little in the way of service to help him stay there.

The irony is that very few people go into institutions without a great deal of reluctance.

The Task Force focused primarily on the use of tax dollars. It acted under cabinet authority, and its recommendations, though kept secret from the public for two years, were relied on by government. The report was no academic exercise, but a venture into the world of costs balanced against benefits in the context of an ever tightened budget. In this connection, it is worth noting that much of the report centred on "the feasibility of equalizing financial recoveries from individuals in residential care facilities," that is, the problem of how to get residents to pay a larger share of the cost of housing them.

Government sought a better balance between what it pays in support of the aged and what the aged could pay in support of themselves. To achieve this balance involves three groups of figures: (a) the amount that government pays in extended care; (b) the amount that the aged receive as guaranteed income under federal and provincial programmes; (c) the comfort allowance an individual is allowed by the province each month regardless of that person's ability to pay residential charges.

Extended care is only one part of a health insurance package available to all Canadians, which is funded in part by premiums from taxes, with the remainder paid as contributions from the provincial and federal governments. (The amount of government contribution is as low as 40 to 45 per cent in Ontario and as high as 90 to 95 per cent in Newfoundland.) Each provincial government determines the level of care it will make available under the scheme. Obviously, the greater the level of care, the greater will be the size of the government's contribution. The contrast between "wealthy" provinces such as Ontario, British Colum-

bia, Alberta, and less affluent provinces such as Newfoundland, Nova
Scotia or New Brunswick, is marked. For the less affluent provinces,
extended care is defined in minimum terms. This is what the "poor"
provinces did *not* provide their older residents in 1969-1970 through
insured payments:
— No optometric examination
— No chiropractic treatment
— No X-rays
— No osteopathic treatment
— No podiatric treatment
— No naturopathic treatment
— No physiotherapy
— No special nursing
Government has cast the national health care scheme as a form of
insurance, not a charity. People understand that they are paying for what
they receive; nothing is handed to them. The insurance programme
gives Canadians a sense of relief from the danger of being financially
destroyed in the event of a serious, long-term illness. And they are
further reassured that health care is sponsored by the government which
monitors both quality and cost of medical care. So long as people know
that government is operating in their best interests, all is well: The high
cost of medical treatment is shared by the entire community thereby
spreading the expense among many, rather than a few, and they receive
a generally high level of quality for their money.

Government, however, has budget limitations and conflicting demands on its resources. The "poor" provinces of Canada illustrate the
point. There government has no choice but to limit extended care
services. The population is poor and tax moneys scarce. And, of course,
government has other services to maintain — welfare, police, fire,
water, utilities and roads. Granted that the old are entitled to share in
government funds. The point is that there must be sharing proportionate
to a province's other needs.

The "poor" provinces are not alone in this dilemma. Ontario, British
Columbia and Alberta all have "budget constraints." The difference
between the rich and poor governments of Canada is one of degree, not
of kind. When the Ontario minister of community and social services
told a Windsor audience in March 1977 that the government "can no
longer afford" to take care of senior citizens "abandoned by their
families," it was not unexpected. In the past, the minister said, government's approach was to build facilities to care for those in need. This
could no longer be done. "Unless people are prepared to pay horrend-

ously high taxes, there is no way we can afford to maintain the level of services we now have. . . . If a family has a member in a wheelchair, for instance, and needs to renovate their home in order to accommodate it, we can provide the money. I'd rather see that than see the handicapped person have to leave the home.''

In Ontario, just as a freeze has been placed on the development of new chronic hospital facilities, there is no significant growth in the number of extended care beds. Indeed, there can be no new extended care beds unless a licence is first obtained from the government. And if the number of beds kept at roughly the same level, government will be able not only to blunt the inflationary cost spiral, but properly insist on making (extended care beds available only for those in need of continuing nursing.) All this can be done (and is being done) without changing or enacting new laws or regulations.

Squeezing the Old: New Charges[3]

The matter does not end with a freeze on new extended care beds. Ontario already has a substantial number of extended care beds and their cost is high.)In 1975 the Ontario Interministerial Committee reported to the cabinet: ''At present there is no overall policy regarding charges to individuals in residential care facilities. A broad range of practices exist — from situations in which no direct charge is made against the client as all services are covered by health insurance, to situations in which facilities attempt to recover all of the costs from the client, or his family.'' The committee mentioned a number of different kinds of facilities housing the aged and stressed the lack of any coordinated policy concerning charges and reimbursement (of which extended care is a major part). The committee argued for planning and control and posed questions that reflect the conflicting demands on government resources:

- Why should those who are resident in a home for the aged be treated differently regarding costs from those in a home for special care?
- Why should residents in homes for the aged be treated differently as to costs from extended care clients in the same home?
- Why should different facilities (that is, homes for special care and psychiatric hospitals) providing essentially the same care impose different charges?

These questions have no satisfactory answers. A resident in a (chronic care hospital who receives a minimum of 76 hours of nursing care each month pays nothing for room, board or health care. This contrasts sharply with the resident in a home for the aged who is billed an average of $360 each month for residential care) Similarly, (a wealthy resident supported by extended care in a home for the aged pays about one half of the average amount billed a person in residential care in the same home.) Many more incongruities exist.

But bureaucracy alone did not bring about this fantasy world of finance. (The legislature too must bear the responsibility for confusion and conflict.) Charitable organizations have a long-standing interest in the care of the aged, and government has supported that interest. Much of their budgets, both for building construction and maintenance, is paid for by the government. Still, a small percentage (about 20 per cent) of a charitable institution's annual operating budget must be raised by the institution itself. What is not obtained by fund-raising drives must come from charges to the residents themselves. The result is that those who happen to live in a home run by a charitable institution are likely to pay more for their maintenance) than those in a home for the aged. Yet both institutions perform precisely the same function.

Clearly, in Ontario the government is moving toward "uniform" financial policy on residential services for the aged. An essential element of that policy will require residents to pay a flexible portion of the costs of their maintenance. In the 1975 study the Ontario government surveyed sixty private board-and-lodging facilities. It found that the monthly cost for room and board varied between $150 and $215. For extended care residents in homes for the aged or nursing homes, the average daily amount required from individuals is $5.90, or $177 per month. (With the same moneys they could obtain room and board in the community.) More striking, however, are the amounts charged for intermediate or residential care in the same facilities: there, residents or their families are obligated to pay $12 to $15 each day for a total of $360 to $450 each month — figures far in excess of what private lodging houses were charging.

(Government sets the rates) that homes for the aged or nursing homes may charge, directly pays these institutions for each extended care patient, and there is no doubt that its bill is large and growing. What remains questionable is just how much of government's outlay is wastage; in other words, how much does it *really* cost to maintain a resident in a home for the aged or a nursing home? How much of what the government pays or, for that matter, what a resident pays goes to maintain that resident?

Nursing homes in Ontario have more than 26,000 beds, most of which are designated as extended care. The government increased the amount that the homes could charge extended care residents ($5.90), in addition to the amount the homes received from health insurance coverage, in order to compel a senior citizen to hand over to a home the increases he or she obtained as a result of a new provincial pension programme, the Guaranteed Annual Income System (GAINS) (see page 83). How much of that increase went to pay for services rendered the resident is another matter. Indeed, it is fair to say that government seems singularly uninterested — in its public statements — in nursing home profits. Yet the same government collects detailed data on this subject. The questions, however, remain. In 1977 the Ontario Nursing Home Association, the trade association for the Ontario nursing homes, stated that the "bulk raw food cost" daily for each resident is $1.50 to $1.80. The association also estimated that 60 to 65 per cent of the nursing homes' total expenses pays the salaries of the employees — generally unskilled or semi-skilled.

In 1977 the Ontario government released its 1975 interministerial study to stimulate public discussion of the high cost of institutionalizing the aged. While the study makes clear what government is spending and what homes are receiving, what is not made clear is just how the money received is being used. And it seems that government has no intention of informing the public how those moneys are used. More particularly, government will not release even generalized data about profit levels of nursing homes — profits obtained entirely from taxpayers' money. In response to an enquiry from the Ontario ombudsman concerning profits, the deputy minister of health wrote of the need to maintain secrecy in the interest of nursing homes. Information, he said, would be released if government by law ordered its release:

> As a general policy, my Ministry believes that information pertaining to the private affairs of the citizen, and revealed to the Ministry pursuant to a requirement of statute or regulation, ought not to be disclosed by the Ministry except in the context of the administration of that statute or regulation — or, at the most, the administration of associated Ministry legislation.
> The basis of this policy is two-fold:
> 1. The right of the citizen to expect that he will hold in confidence any information compulsorily disclosed by him to us; and
> 2. Our dependence on the untrammeled flow of such information to us, and our consequent need not to treat it in a manner that might prejudice future candor.

(It has been indicated) that the information sought may be in a form which does not identify the specific informants; in my opinion this consideration would not obviate the necessity for the application of our general policy, since the individual informant has a stake in the collective information of which his specific information forms a part. . . .

No one would dispute . . . that public discussion of ideas is in the public interest, but that proposition standing by itself is not very helpful. Again, while in a general sense it is desirable that useful information be provided to the public, we consider that a bald statement of that kind without regard for all the attendant circumstances does very little to come to grips with the specific problem.

The public discussion referred to by the deputy minister was urged by the government itself. It was government which wanted the public to discuss the high cost of institutionalizing the aged. It was government which provided some of the essential data relating to those costs. And it was government which chose to eliminate the remaining facts — how money spent is used — from the public debate, inside and outside the legislature.

The deputy minister did provide the ombudsman with some information. In response to queries concerning nursing home profit figures, after initially denying that such information even existed, the deputy minister submitted the form which nursing home operators must regularly complete, and which requires details of all the information needed to determine profit.

The public discussion on institutionalization of the aged in Ontario, then, was to become a means for government to bring the public to a conclusion which it had already reached. On the other hand, the public was to know only enough to be supportive of already determined government policy.

Passing the Buck: Letting Ottawa Pay[4]

The core of that policy is directed (toward saving money for the provincial government.) Its strategy is keyed to existing *federal* spending: the federal government is paying most Canadians over 65 a minimum pension through Old Age Security (OAS) and the Guaranteed Income Supplement (GIS). (OAS and GIS are available to bring the entire population aged 65 and older to at least a poverty level of income.) Neither OAS nor GIS are based on premium payments or involvement in the work force. Rather, they (are conditional only on residence in

Canada, age, and (for GIS) income level. In the 1970s nearly half of those Canadians over 65 were drawing GIS. In the past few years both plans have been somewhat modified to respond to inflationary pressures; as the dollar decreases in value, the amount paid out in OAS and GIS will increase to maintain mimimum purchasing power.

In addition to OAS and GIS, is a social insurance scheme called the Canada Pension Plan (CPP). This is available to those who have worked until the age of 65 and, over the years, have contributed to the plan. The amount of the CPP depends on individual contributions (which include those of the employer). Until recently men and women in receipt of CPP were, in effect, penalized if they worked after the age of 65; they lost a portion of their CPP once their post-65 income exceeded a certain amount. Under 1974 amendments to the CPP that punitive condition was eliminated. Those over 65 and lucky enough to find paying jobs may draw their full CPP and retain their position in the community like any other citizen.

The CPP, combined with OAS, was designed to ensure life with dignity for those over 65. Certainly, for some the social insurance scenario after 65 might be bright: government provides a basic level of support, and if the individual has a private pension, it is stacked on top of OAS and CPP. If, in addition, (the person can find some part-time employment, the salary will nicely supplement an already adequate income.) This is the ideal.

Reality, however, is different, and government knows this. Most (Canadians do *not* have private pensions,) and those who do, for various reasons, very often will (never receive the benefits.) That is why the government of Ontario, a province which pioneered in private pension protection, in the 1977 Speech from the Throne declared that it "will appoint a Royal Commission on Pension Plans to make an in-depth review and assessment of pension plan administration throughout Ontario. This step will be taken with a view toward necessary changes or other approaches to ensure that contributors receive fair benefit and protection."

In OAS and GIS the government of Ontario saw an opportunity:(the province could *add* to the two federal programmes. A little more money for all might enable individuals to remain in their homes, limit expansion of residences for the aged, and even begin to recoup more money from those residents.)

So the Ontario Guaranteed Annual Income System (GAINS), administered by the Ministry of Revenue, became operative in 1977. By January of that year GAINS provided assurance of an annual individual income of $3,352.20 for Ontario residents over 65, and $6,704.40 for married couples.)The GAINS cheque represents the diffeence between any income the individual (or couple) had in the previous calendar year and the provincial monthly guarantee of $279.35. (In addition, a wider group than those eligible for OAS and GIS receives GAINS because of more lenient provincial residence requirements for eligibility.)

In 1977 a provincial deputy minister said of GAINS:

> It is working. Fewer older people are going into institutions than might have but for GAINS. They want to stay in the community, and GAINS is allowing them to do so: Don't ask me for statistics. We have done no study. Remember we are politicians. We kind of keep our finger to the wind. We know what is happening and we are glad. Our programme is successful.

A more concrete statement had come in an interministerial memorandum dated April 14, 1975:

> Introduction of the GAINS program had implications for many residential care clients. GAINS payments were intended to(assist low income aged persons in the community to meet high living costs.) If GAINS benefits had been passed on to persons whose needs were already being met through residential care programs at little or, in some cases, no charge, multiple subsidization would have occurred.
>
> This problem was resolved in part by the introduction of increases in the Extended Care co-insurance rate. [This is the amount the individual must pay each day in addition to that paid by Extended Care.] However, some multiple subsidization continued as GAINS benefits were paid to clients in other residential facilities.
>
> This situation, in turn, raised questions concerning the possibility of introducing a universal recovery charge to all residential care clients. That is, a flat rate charge to cover the costs of "room and board" in these facilities.

Levying a universal charge has a nice administrative-financial logic. It does not, however,(meet special needs.) This the 1975 interministerial report recognized when it argued for a "broad charging policy which is sufficiently flexible to accommodate differences in [institutional] orientation, program objections and client characteristics." If such a policy were adopted, the report recommended two alternative approaches toward its implementation:

— Develop a charging policy as one element of a "wider, overall re-assessment of residential care policies and practices." In this regard, the charging policy must reflect the fundamental orientation and goals of residential care programmes.

— Or develop a step-by-step approach of charging on a "target group basis within existing constraints."

In other words, the report recommended the government should either (a) revamp the entire institutional structure of care for the aged and in that setting develop a charging policy which would be supportive of the new structure; or (b) keep the existing structure but rationalize the charging policy by eliminating gross inequities. As might be expected, government took a little from both recommendations without publicly committing itself to either.

As fundamental policy, government began to make it more difficult for persons to come into extended care and, at the same time, increased somewhat the individual cost for those already covered by it. In its step-by-step approach, government is paving the way to "rationalize" the discretionary allowance.[5] In March 1975 extended care residents received $92.80 each month as discretionary income while those having only residential care were given only $70.98.

The 1975 interministerial report had raised a number of questions, all concerned with the already small amount of discretionary income:

— What is the reason for large variations in the discretionary *incomes of the aged?*

— Why does it increase as health deteriorates?

— Why does discretionary income increase the further one moves from self-sufficient community living? For an old person in the community to have $51 of discretionary income (the level of a person in extended care in a home for the aged), he would have to feed, clothe and shelter himself for $179 a month.

— Why does the discretionary income of some residents rise and fall frequently? The discretionary income of extended care residents is the difference between GAINS and the extended care charge. Since GAINS escalates quarterly and the extended care rate changes less frequently, the discretionary income of the extended care cases is subject to wide fluctuations. (In comparison, the comfort allowance of $43 — for example, to residential care cases in homes for the aged — is subject to infrequent periodic adjustment.)

— Why are some items — reading matter, toiletries, clothing — provided free in certain homes for the aged and charged for in others?

— Should current discretionary incomes in homes for the aged and nursing homes be reduced?

To sum up, then, the policy of the Ontario government is clear even though it has never been fully expressed to the electorate:

— The guaranteed income programme has been fashioned (to keep older people out of institutions)

— It will become more difficult for individuals to qualify for extended care. Admission will tend to be centralized; control will be taken away from family physicians and nursing homes.

— Those who are institutionalized will no longer find themselves favoured financially over those who are not. As far as they are able, institutionalized persons, and especially those in extended care, will be required to pay for that care. If those who enter a home on extended care have personal assets, it is altogether possible that government will *compel* their use to help to pay for room and board. In any event, government can be sure to cut the size of discretionary (comfort) allowances available to home residents.

No one could complain if the core of government policy were to return the individual to the community or, in the first instance, to keep the old in their neighbourhoods, but the objection is that saving is the motivating factor and, once this is achieved, government considers it need do no more.

The truth is that much more might be done. Will wealthy Ontario, having saved money through its GAINS programme, opt to develop another programme of home care? A 1974 long-term report on health care urged this (but the same report spoke of minimal cost savings):

> A number of studies in Canada and observation of services actually established, particularly in the Western Provinces, suggests that services like visiting nurses, home help, handyman or woman, meals-on-wheels, house cleaning, visiting, telephone callers, pension, legal and tax counselling, etc., could help many elderly persons remain in their own homes where the majority of them prefer to be. These services are poorly developed in some Ontario centres and virtually not at all in most. Studies suggest the overall cost would be markedly less than institutional care and that cost could be controlled by relating non-residential services to specific groups rather than making them universal.

These recommendations of the 1974 report have not been implemented. A cost-conscious government dares not take the risk. It is enough for such a government to blunt the increasing flow of the aged into institutions. And stemming, not eliminating, the flow of the aged to institutions is all that government *can* achieve, because the government itself is responsible for developing the specialized interest groups who will lobby for institutionalization, because they depend upon it for their very survival. Nursing homes and old age homes will not be put out of business. (Government policy will only restrain their growth,) just as it did in the case of chronic care hospitals in 1972.

a portfolio of photographs by Andrew Danson

1

2

3

4

6

7

8

1 A 93-year-old retired piano teacher (left) with her sister an 87-year-old retired theater manager, just prior to their move into a nursing home. Their family was paying a hundred dollars a day in home care costs, and had no choice but to make the decision for them.

2 A grandmother in her seventies, tending to her egg stall in the farmers' market, with granddaughter.

3 A 78-year-old grandmother at her weekly bowling session.

4 Woman at a New Horizon community card party.

5 A semi-retired farmers' market operator with his son, who now runs the business.

6 A retired justice of the peace, 85 years old.

7 An 80-year-old man who lives alone, deals in antiques and sells pigs.

8 Three neighbours who live alone and independently from one another in a small Ontario community. Their ages range from 80 to 94 years.

CHAPTER SEVEN

The Physician and the Coroner

What a curious state of affairs that the coroner, an officer concerned with death, is the only instrument for questioning medical standards designed to protect the living.

Protection after Death[1]

But for the coroner, the death of 61-year-old Bertha Richardson probably would have passed unnoticed. She was, after all, a bedridden older person who had been treated intermittently for more than two years in an acute care hospital before being moved to a nursing home where she died about six weeks later. Not that she died in the nursing home itself; few patients do. After her condition had deteriorated, she was sent from the nursing home to a hospital. It was there that she died.

To the lay person the medical cause of her death means little. The death certificate stated that she died of bilateral bronchopneumonia, complicated by bleeding oesophageal varices which were pulapsed due to micronodular cirrhosis of the liver. Mrs. Richardson's family and friends, facing the technical language of medicine, could say little.

It was another matter for the Coroner's Office whose motto is: "We speak for the dead to protect the living." The death of every resident in a nursing home or home for the aged must be reported to the coroner. As in England for over a thousand years, the coroner has to ask these fundamental questions:

— Who is the deceased?
— Where did she die?
— How did she come to her death?
— When did she die?
— By what means did she die?

In the case of Mrs. Richardson all of the questions except the last were easy to answer. The final question required the coroner to determine more than whether Mrs. Richardson died from natural causes. He had to determine whether those causes were "preventable", that is, if Mrs. Richardson had received reasonable care, would she have died at that time? He also had to "alert forces in the community" to cope with the root causes of death. This includes conditions in the community itself which may contribute to death.

The coroner, a physician himself, appointed another physician in his office, Dr. Margaret Milton, to conduct an enquiry. Dr. Milton, who once before had unsuccessfully sought an industry-wide inquiry into the quality of medical care in nursing homes, called for an autopsy and a Coroner's Court to hold an inquest. The court was composed of four lay persons whose function was not to find individual guilt, but rather to hear evidence, make findings of fact, and recommendations to the coroner which, if implemented, might prevent other deaths from occurring in quite the same way.

In Ontario, as in most other jurisdictions, the office of coroner is part of the administration of justice. The coroner comes under the Public Safety Division of the Ministry of the Solicitor General. The Coroner's Office functions ''in the interests of the welfare and the safety of the community.''

The discretion given the coroner does not always mean that it will be exercised. Searching investigations are the exception, not the rule. In any superficial inquiry the death of Mrs. Richardson could easily have been ascribed to natural causes which were not preventable.

In 1960 more than 1,300 inquests were held in Ontario, a number far in excess of most other jurisdictions. By 1972 the province had 380 coroners who investigated 25,000 deaths (40 per cent of the total number of deaths in the province). Eight thousand and five hundred autopsies and 600 inquests resulted from their investigations. By 1974 the number of deaths investigated rose to 27,000, but the number of autopsies declined to 8,175 and inquests dropped to 306. For reasons of economy the coroner had decided to cut back. It costs $150 for a ''basic'' autopsy, and more extensive tests can increase the cost to $250. [2]

Money is but one pressure. Any full investigation touching government brings the coroner into potential conflict not only with vested interests, but with government itself. For example, Metropolitan Toronto Coroner Dr. Morton Shulman did not hesitate to use his office to bring about reform. Not infrequently, however, reform was fought, and the coroner's investigations became confrontations. (Dr. Shulman wrote of these encounters in *Coroner*.)[3]

Dr. Shulman did not long remain chief coroner of Metropolitan Toronto. His tenure brought political turmoil, and when he left office to become an opposition gadfly to the government, it was abundantly clear that his successor would take a more conservative line. The new chief coroner seemed to define his function in terms of the proximate causes of death as seen by a doctor. Only with temerity was ''community reform'' made an object of a Coroner's Court. That is why the inquest and Coroner's Court inquiry into the death of Mrs. Richardson is so remarkable.

Caring for One Person: Doctors on Review[4]

The inquest into the death of Mrs. Richardson was held even though her death and the quality of her treatment were not unusual. There were no flagrant violations of Ontario regulations. However, it is fair to say that the standard of medical care in Quebec's "underground" makes the licensed homes in Ontario seem like secure havens. The *Montreal Star* reported in 1976 that there often is *no* medical care for residents in some of the more than 200 underground homes. One Quebec nursing home director falsely represented himself as a doctor. He gave unnecessary injections to diabetic patients. He promised both patients and their families that there would be skilled medical therapy, and there was next to nothing. Four times his home was "closed" by government, and four times it remained open.

Nor is the situation better in the United States. A study group of Consumer Advocate Ralph Nader made this evaluation, which seems particularly applicable to the death of Mrs. Richardson:

> It is obvious that no single kind of medical treatment facility can meet the needs of the aged. Some need intensive hospital care; others need round-the-clock custodial care; still others need only a pair of younger legs to run out and buy the groceries. Yet there is almost no flexibility in the present system. Hospitals are over-crowded, and so expensive as to place them out of reach for many of the aged. One million elderly people are in some twenty-four thousand nursing homes across the country; but this is only 5 per cent of the aged population, and nursing homes are so crowded and generally provide such miserable care that it is impossible to conceive of their taking care of more people. For the other 95 per cent, the alternatives are few indeed. Home nursing services are costly and hard to find, especially in nonurban areas; community housing is practically nonexistent; anyone who has tried to arrange care for an aged relative knows that all forms of noninstitutional care are woefully lacking. *So bad is the situation that an official of the Department of Health, Education, and Welfare told us that on any given day 50 percent of the aged are in the wrong place; if they are in a hospital, they should be in a nursing home; if in a nursing home, they should be at home, and so forth* [C. Townsend, *Old Age:The Last Segregation*, 1971].

The inquest established the facts. Mrs. Richardson had been transferred from an acute care hospital to a nursing home, where she was given a medical examination and certain blood tests were made. There was no evidence of any violence directed toward her. Nor was there any evidence that she was treated differently from other patients in the eleven-person room. Like the others, Mrs. Richardson was confined to her bed. Just as soon as her condition worsened she was transferred to a hospital where facilities were available for better treatment; the nursing home had limited equipment and personnel. It could be said that the nursing home was not materially different from other nursing homes in the province.

From admission to death, however, Mrs. Richardson did not appear to be the first concern of those who treated her. This is not to say that anyone intended to harm her nor that there was gross negligence. Mrs. Richardson simply was in the way: a person to be moved from an expensive acute care hospital bed to a less expensive facility. That burden fell on a hospital social worker. She understood the difficulty in finding space — any space — for an older person on a long-term basis. She did what was necessary to get Mrs. Richardson into a nursing home. Nimble draftsmanship in responding to nursing home admission forms was her forte. It was not overly important that the forms, as completed, did not fully convey the state of Mrs. Richardson's condition or needs.

Though the coroner, Dr. Milton, had some rather strong words for what the hospital social worker did — and the nursing home's reliance on those statements — she was not entirely to blame. With the admission forms had come a detailed medical history in which Mrs. Richardson's physicians had stated the nature of her treatment and offered suggestions for further care. She clearly had received excellent medical attention in the acute care hospital.

Although, once admitted to the nursing home, Mrs. Richardson was examined by a home physician, it is questionable whether the nursing home physician understood fully the extent of her past medical history and her present needs. Moreover, though he ordered laboratory tests, the results did not come until several days later. Earlier reporting would have brought a clearer understanding of Mrs. Richardson's condition. Dr. Milton asked: "What in God's name is the use of sending transfer papers from a highly recognized hospital if they're going to be ignored?"

Mrs. Richardson was not singled out for good, bad or indifferent treatment. She was one of eleven in one room. Her ten room-mates were also bedridden and in need of medical attention. They might have been classified as "senile" by the home administration, but to Dr. Milton they had feelings: ". . . [I]t is a harrowing experience for a Coroner to walk into a room where there are four, six, or eight patients. You find one bed curtained off, obviously waiting for the Coroner to come. You have twelve eyes watching you as you walk down the room. . . . It may be said that these patients are 'senile,' but believe me they know when someone has died. Their eyes show me they are afraid. They wonder if they are going to be next."

Addressing the jury, Dr. Milton said that Mrs. Richardson's death was not "atypical": "It takes a case such as this to really emphasize what can happen. . . . After reviewing the case I really felt that this was a preventable death, and it could have happened to any other 61-year-old woman. Regardless of the fact that she had illnesses, regardless of all this, in my opinion it was a preventable death had she received proper, adequate care. . . ."

The coroner's jury then had to determine: What was the standard of medical care for Mrs. Richardson? What ought to have been the standard of medical care? What was the role of government in ensuring that an agreed standard of care was met?

The four jurors could have begun with Hippocrates, who said: "In order to cure the human body it is necessary to have knowledge of the whole of things." It was not merely enough to understand Mrs. Richardson's narrow medical needs; it was important to understand her total needs. Certainly, no one had troubled to understand Mrs. Richardson's total needs. She had fundamental problems that a team of five physicians who took turns in their weekly visits to the nursing home simply could not grasp. The team, faced with a heavy work load, did their best, but that was not good enough for Dr. Milton: "Physicians earn enough to spend some extra time in behalf of these institutions. . . ."

Differences that Count[5]

The coroner's jury found a precedent in the application of the Hippocratic oath. They also found a precedent in the formal regulations governing "The Duties of a Physician to a Home for the Aged" in Ontario. This document provides: "By accepting the appointment of Physician to a Home for the Aged, the physician indicates that he or she intends to give the residents the same good medical practice he or she would accord his or her private patients, *and in addition assumes the following responsibilities. . . .''* By accepting an appointment as a physician in a provincially run home for the aged, the doctor has to give care that *exceeds* the normal standard. The regulations leave no doubt that the physician must be concerned with the residents' full welfare, a concept that even embraces the general home environment. However viewed, the regulations far exceed the standard of medical care given Mrs. Richardson. It is even possible that if that standard of practice had been applied, Mrs. Richardson, who suffered from a lack of potassium, would have lived.

In the first instance, a physician at a home for the aged is *required* to examine not only the applications for admission, but also the supporting medical documents. What Mrs. Richardson's doctors in the acute care hospital said and recommended would have to be reviewed by the doctor in the admitting home.

Moreover, the same doctor is required to examine the applicant herself *thoroughly*. Laboratory tests must be made quickly and efficiently. No delay of the kind to which Mrs. Richardson was subjected is tolerated. Further, if Mrs. Richardson needed medication which the home could not safely provide (including a follow-up assessment of side effects) or if she required a standard of general care not available in the home, it is the obligation of the home physician to recommend rejection of the application for admission. Mrs. Richardson would never have been admitted to a home for the aged (a government-run home) which did not understand her medical condition and could not adequately serve her.

Once admitted to a home, residents will find doctors who make rounds once or twice weekly, and "provide emergency service so . . . [that they are available] at all times in case of sudden illness, accident or death.'' Annually the same doctors will give all the old people complete medical examinations. The results of these findings will be recorded and put in each resident's medical file, and these files are maintained in such a way that other home physicians can use them. When necessary (and it is the doctor's duty to so determine) vaccinations or inoculations (with residents' consent) may be ordered.

Home physicians have another obligation: they are required to become active participants, principals, in controlling and shaping the general home environment. The government regulations to which the physicians at Ontario homes for the aged subscribe require them:

— To submit an annual report to the Home Board of Management on the health of the residents and recommendations for improvements (even outside the medical field) which could enhance the welfare of the residents.

— To be aware of environmental factors in the Home, e.g., temperature and humidity, influencing the health and comfort of the residents, and to make such recommendations to the administration as he deems essential.

— To maintain a sympathetic interest in and cooperate with . . . all reactivation programs carried on by paramedical personnel.

— To supervise the dietary programs of the Home and the nutritional state of all residents . . . as a primary consideration of the Home physician.

— Where a resident is involved in an accident, together with the Home nursing supervisor to determine by history and examination the character and extent of the injury and initiate any appropriate treatment.

The standards for physicians at Ontario homes for the aged are only partly applicable to those doctors treating nursing home residents. The most important difference is one of commitment. Physicians at homes for the aged have agreed to commit themselves to the residents' general welfare. They have agreed as professionals, as people concerned with healing others, to serve as surrogates of the public in the home for the aged. As physicians, they are required to exercise judgment independently of the home administration, and they direct these judgments to what is necessary for the total welfare of the resident; their authority includes and goes beyond the residents' mere medical needs.

The jury enquiring into the death of Mrs. Richardson were made aware that some standards did exist controlling medical care in institutions for the aged, but the jurors had to come to their own conclusions. They listened to four days of testimony and a lengthy charge from the coroner. Then the jury retired and deliberated for more than six hours. Like all juries, they deliberated alone. They were not guided by professionals. The verdict and recommendations were theirs alone. Dr. Milton made suggestions, but stated clearly that they were in no way binding.

The jurors listened to the testimony surrounding the death of Mrs. Richardson as *citizens*, but in their official capacity as members of a jury brought back a verdict — that Mrs. Richardson died of natural causes which were preventable — and four handwritten pages of recommendations designed to prevent similar deaths from occurring in future, and to improve the quality of life in nursing homes. The Toronto

Globe and Mail in an editorial praised the jury as "unusually diligent," and noted the basic points in its sixteen recommendations. The recommendations were:

1. The existing system of patient transfer from Acute Treatment Hospitals to Chronic Hospitals, Senior Citizen Homes, Nursing Homes, etc., should be completely revised, to include the following:

    (a) An Admission Committee should be formed by the Receiving Institution. This Committee shall consist of a Physician, Nurse, and possibly an Aid or Recreation Director. At least one member of the Committee should visit the patient prior to admission.

    (b) The original copy of the Medical Assessment Form, which is attached to the Application for Admission, must be kept by the Hospital.

    (c) All sections of the Medical Assessment Form must be signed by the parties concerned — i.e. the Physician, Head Nurse, and Social Worker. Great care should be taken that the patient's condition is accurately described.

    (d) The Social Worker should not have the responsibility for. . .acceptance of a patient into any Nursing Home.

    (e) The Social Worker should advise the Relatives of a patient to visit the proposed Home.

2. Hospital Departments of Social Work . . . must ensure that adequate records, pertaining to Social Workers' contacts with patients, relatives, and Nursing Homes are maintained.

3. A committee from the College of Physicians and Surgeons, the Coroner's Office, and the Medical Association of Ontario, should be formed to study medical care standards at [the home where Mrs. Richardson was taken], and Nursing Homes, in general.

4. Attending Physicians at the Nursing Home, must sign the medical instructions that are sent along with the patient, signifying receipt of the instructions.

5. The Advisory Physician should serve as an Administrative Physician and coordinate all medical services within the Home to ensure adequate medical care standards and procedures are being followed. He should exclude himself from active case work.

6. A member of the regular group of attending Physicians should be on call for nights and weekends, rather than an outside service.

7. The building construction and accommodation standards for Nursing homes should include:

    (a) privacy curtains around each bed in a multi-bed room;

(b) a bed lamp on each bed;   ·
(c) a working call bell on each bed (a manual one if above is out of order);
(d) limiting the number of beds per room to six;
(e) definition of the recreation director's role to include contact with bed-ridden patients, as well as activities for the ambulatory. Provision should be made (probably with the help of Volunteers) so each patient can be assisted in personal matters such as shopping, letter writing, etc., or just provide a listening ear. All rooms should have some homey touches, such as colourful drapes, plants, pictures, etc.

Compliance with these standards be included as part of the Ontario Health Ministry Inspection.

8. Emphasis should be placed in locating patients in rooms where they may have congenial company, and promote every possibility where patients can help each other, or do little jobs around the Home.

9. [Government] inspection visits should be made on strictly a random basis, rather than the approximately regular inspections presently carried out.

10. The deceased should be removed from a multi-bed room immediately, to an unoccupied room.

11. The Chief Coroner should instruct all Coroners to service Nursing Homes within two hours of receiving notification of a death.

12. Coroners should be included in the inspection of Nursing Homes with detailed reports submitted to the Chief Coroner.

13. Laboratories should call Physician immediately upon knowledge of gross abnormalities in the results of tests.

14. A Central Referral Centre for Nursing Homes should be established to
(a) collect data on each Nursing Home in the area
(b) provide information on vacancies
(c) provide publications listing and describing information on each Nursing Home, to be available to the public as well as professionals.

15. Personnel responsible for referring patients to Nursing Homes should make a tour of all Nursing Homes in the area, at least once a year.

16. Nursing Home personnel should be aware of free outside services, such as Canadian National Institute for the Blind, Public Library Shut-In Service, Hospital Auxiliary, Local Church help, etc.

The recommendations of the coroner's jury do not have the force of law. They do not speak of individual fault and, as such, they bring no threat of imprisonment or fine or even civil action. The recommendations of the coroner's jury enquiring into the death of Mrs. Richardson were received by Dr. Milton for transfer to the chief coroner and the crown attorney. At most, the recommendations had persuasive value.

Yet, for all its limitations, the Coroner's Office was a place of last resort. Dr. Milton said to her jury:

> Remember, it is only after Mrs. Richardson's death that a medical doctor took the time to listen, to investigate and study the care of this patient. And that person is a Coroner. There is no other doctor to whom [a concerned person] could turn. . . . Take away the Coroner and you are left with a letter of complaint to the [Government inspection branch dealing with nursing homes, which enforces nursing standards, but not those relating to a doctor]. Or [there could be a letter] to a Member of Parliament or maybe a letter to the Minister of Health. But you don't have any personal contact. It is lost in the bureaucracy. While a person is living, it is very difficult for a patient or relative, as you have learned in these past few days, to complain to a doctor in a nursing home or to the administrator. I put it to you: This is the existing system.

Ontario considers itself a province which sets good standards for its nursing homes and homes for the aged. On the Canadian scene, and indeed in a North American context, Ontario certainly holds a high position in relation to other jurisdictions. Yet in Ontario there are no medical standards for nursing homes set by legislation nor are such standards set indirectly. The Medical Society for Ontario remains removed. The government-subsidized hospital insurance programme will intervene only if a doctor's billings are out of line or, more generally, once every five years for accreditation purposes. What a curious state of affairs that the coroner, an officer concerned with death, is the only instrument for questioning medical standards designed to protect the living.

CHAPTER EIGHT

New Beginnings

"Don't look on the aged as ever having reached a point of no return. . . .Preserve their identity."
Dr. David Lander

Words from a Country Doctor[1]

In the West he is known as the Doctor Who Cares. His patients call him by his first name, Dr. Dave. The province of Alberta presented him with its first mental health award. For nearly forty years Dr. David Lander practised in the towns of Black Diamond and Turner Valley, the heart of the Alberta oil fields. Dr. Dave never turned patients away; he gave them the attention they needed. And he found that so very often it was attention, not drugs that the patient required.

In 1970 Dr. Dave retired from his oil field practice and began to direct his energies toward the elderly. At that time, and at the age of 62, Dr. Dave became the *first* doctor in Alberta to be concerned primarily with the aged. He publicly chastised the medical profession for placing "geriatrics on the low end of the totem pole." To his fellow doctors he said: "When you treat a young person, you cure him. It makes you feel like God. In old people you are dealing with broken-down material. It is not exciting; you don't see immediate results, most doctors think . . . The second reason is that very little was taught in medical schools about how to deal with old people. And what you don't know, you leave alone. (And that is why) there is not one geriatrician in Alberta."

Dr. Dave might have added a third reason to his list. (To treat the old properly requires attention, sympathy and time, which means money). A doctor has to listen and respond more like a helpful, dutiful son or daughter than to give orders like a mother or father. Dr. Dave said:

> The first thing is to allay fears and anxieties. Then don't look on the aged as ever having reached a point of no return. . . . Preserve their identity. Don't deflate them by calling them by their first name if you have no right. He or she is a personality. . . . Don't lie to patients. Don't give them sugar-coated reassurance, but carefully choose your words. When a doctor says "stroke," an

old person hears paralysis, loss of speech, dependence. Many people recover their abilities. . . . Keep the same routine for dying patients as you have for living ones. Visit the patient. Sit down and talk. Touch him or her. It's bad enough to die, but to feel you are untouchable is unforgivable. Death in a patient is not a failure. It is not a trap and it does not impinge on the doctor's ability. A doctor should help a dying person die comfortably.

To a doctor, however, time is money. It is also energy-draining. To give an injection, prescribe a pill or order a test can be handled quickly. Moreover, the decisions made are based on objective criteria. So it is easier and far more profitable to treat people as machines than to build a personal relationship. For the general practitioner this "conveyor belt" medicine often means turning an office into a clearing house. "Difficult" cases are "farmed out" to specialists who, in turn, treat only the specific complaint. Except perhaps during a general physical examination, general practitioners, or "family" doctors, have little time to talk or, more especially, listen to their patients. After all, doctors' compensation is based on numbers of visits.

To Dr. Dave, money is not the most important criterion in building a practice. To him, it is far more important to centre on his patients' needs. In this regard, Dr. Dave takes a broad view of his function. He has a deep belief in the capacity of people to live — if given the chance and the support. As a doctor, he has taken up the cause of the old, and his words are tough and sharply to the point:

> Some patients in nursing homes just sit there like the sphinx and people think they are senile. But a lot are not senile. They are depressed and over-drugged. . . . For ten cents a day you can keep a person tranquilized. It is much easier. But with the proper medication they can be brought out of their depression and live. . . . Old people in institutions often have their privacy invaded by well-meaning attendants. . . . Some of the most frustrated old people are in nursing homes. What is the matter with holding hands, talking? Sex is not only for procreation. It is for recreation, relief, communication. It is cruel to forbid warmth and affection. . . . Residents ought to have "Do Not Disturb" signs for their doors so that they can do their entertaining in private and in peace. . . . There is no reason why an old person should not feel well. If we cannot cure him, we should be able to relieve him. And if we cannot do that, we can at least comfort him.

Dr. Dave would like to write a Bill of Rights for the old. These rights take the form of securities:

The first is financial security. The next is intellectual security —
and I don't mean a university degree. There are lots of jackasses
around with a diploma. I mean the ability to read and follow
current events. [After that] there is social security. This is not a
cheque, but the knowledge that you are part of a group and loved
or loving. Everyone needs love; if not from a member of the
opposite sex, then God, or your dog or your work. . . . Finally,
spiritual security gives comfort. This is the last rock on which to
stand. Religion is good, if it is belief in a merciful God.

Who is to make fast the securities of which Dr. Dave spoke? The
answer, in part, may rest in other questions: Who has denied the old the
securities sought by Dr. Dave? The old were once young. Didn't the old
have the means to plan? Didn't they have the capacity to set aside
savings for retirement? Couldn't they have planned a future in a community outside of institutions? There are, after all, significant numbers
of elderly persons who have taken their own lives in hand; they take
pride in what they have done and they live outside of institutions . . .
But they know that they are allowed few mistakes. If they sell their
home in the city and move to their cottage in the country, it will be no
easy matter to return, once they discover the loneliness of life on their
own. They know, too, that the future may find them disabled, unable to
care for themselves.

The aged in institutions represent but a small percentage of the total
aged population. Many live there as a result of planning that went awry
or children unable or unwilling to care for them. Age is not a surprise; it
is a process that begins from the date of birth. At different rates, but
ever so surely the body ages.

Many more live in homes because they were never able to plan. Older
women, the largest number of poor in North American society, illustrate
this. In their seventies and eighties they are likely to be widowed and
without a private pension. They lack private income because they have
done what this society encourages: they married, had children and
remained housekeepers dependent on their husbands' income. Yet when
the male head of the household retired, he was lucky to have a private
pension. (Less than 40 per cent of the Canadian work force, in fact,
have private pensions that are really theirs). In any event, on the death
of a male head of a household the private pension would either end or be
substantially cut; and the widow could statistically count on living about
another twelve years — in poverty and alone. Her only choice is life in
an institution. She is dependent on the state and she despairs.

She lacks the means to earn money. She has never been paid for work done. Her children in all probability have moved from the city where she lives. In any case, she does not want to be a burden to them. She knows their guilt; she might even like to relieve it but cannot. The sadness of mothers and children facing that final separation in a nursing home can be overwhelming. In *Warm Are The Memories – Sad Is The Heart*, an unpublished poem, Sandra Andich wrote:

This nursing home seems old and ugly
Perhaps because my feelings are much the same
this first visit
The pace I need to bring me closer to you
is very laboured
My heart feels heavy
My head is pounding so
The closer I come
the farther away I wish I could go
My eyes close, trying desperately
to avoid what I know I must face
Around the corner, I was told she would be
I don't want to go
I don't want to see
"There she is"
Where, where, my eyes searched
The corridor was empty, except for a single chair
where upon sat a lone figure
her back to me
Was this my mother?
I'm afraid to see
though deep in my heart
I want to — I know I must
Those saddened eyes, so bewildered and disoriented
began their strong focus upon my forced smile
The eyes begin to brighten
Yes, there is slight recognition
I try to close my ears
to those strange sounds coming forth from her throat
Her arms lift upwards
The fingers begin to dance
beckoning me close
I lean to go into her arms
my strength gives way, emotions burst

I can't meet her touch, for in my heart,
I ache to return to her womb
Blinded by tears, I force myself away
running through closed doors,
one after another
not knowing where
When I can no longer flee, for walls stop me
from where to go,
my thoughts begin to play havoc with warm,
loving memories of long ago
Rationalization eases into my veins
I know now there is nothing more that can ever be done
These walls will be the only walls to confine her now
Never in her own home will she reign again
A beautiful memory
now swallowed by the rising tide of aged humanity
An enormous heartache for blood of her blood to carry
Is this, I ask
a focus into the years of our own finality?

Here is another voice:

> Gribouillisme is the psychiatrists' name for the attitude that con-
> sists of plunging into old age because of the horror that it inspires.
> The subject exaggerates: because she is rather lame she goes
> through the motions of paralysis; because she is rather deaf, she
> stops listening altogether. The functions that are no longer exer-
> cised degenerate, and by playing the cripple, the subject becomes
> one. It is a widely-spread reaction since many old people are
> justifiably resentful and demanding because they have lost hope.
> They take their revenge upon the outside world by exaggerating
> their infirmity: as we have seen, this often occurs in institutions —
> since they have been abandoned, they abandon themselves and
> refuse to make the slightest effort. As this tendency is not checked
> — no one looks after them — many end up by being bedridden
> [Simone de Beauvoir, *The Coming of Age,* 1973].

In such a setting it is too much to demand that the old should care for
themselves. It is too little for the state to provide marginal financial
support and expect the old to live and not merely survive. This is not to
minimize the need for adequate financial support; the development of a
higher government-secured income would enable elderly people to live
outside institutions. By April 1977, Alberta guaranteed individual incomes amounting to $285 a month for the elderly; Ontario and British

Columbia, $279 a month; Saskatchewan, $260 a month; Manitoba, $248 a month; and Nova Scotia, $100 *annually*. The level of income, however, even for the most "generous" of the provinces is not overly great. At the rate of $285 a month no elderly person is going to live in an elegant style in Alberta; at best, he or she will be brought somewhat above the poverty line. The incomes must be larger if the aged are to be kept from drifting into institutions. They must feel, as Dr. Dave stressed, that they have the financial and emotional muscle to survive, not that it would be easier to surrender themselves to an institution and let others care for them.

Being Free[2]

Many do try to maintain themselves until death. They try to remain in their own homes and to live those final years and days fully. The Trotscha family in Toronto intended to do this. Mr. Trotscha, a former cabinetmaker from Rumania, was 64 years old. He and his wife Elizabeth had been married for 31 years when bone cancer caused his terminal illness. Mr. Trotscha wanted to spend his final months at home. His wife agreed; she felt "good about it. . . . I didn't desert him when he was healthy and I wasn't going to desert him when he was sick."

From February 4 to March 11, 1977 all went well. Ontario home care provided a hospital bed which Mr. Trotscha needed, but could not rent on his monthly pension of $398, the couple's total income. On March 11, however, the home care agency threatened to take away the bed. The reason: under agency regulations Mr. Trotscha was no longer eligible for home care. His physician certified the obvious: Mr. Trotscha's condition would not improve; it had "stabilized." Government regulations provide for home care when "the patient's professional treatment is reasonably expected to result in patient progress toward established goals for rehabilitation. *When progress is no longer apparent, the patient is transferred to an alternate and appropriate mode of care.*"

Ministry bureaucrats were unwilling to pay $20 a month, the charge for renting the hospital bed the family kept in the living room of their small two-storey home. But the same bureaucrats were willing to transfer Mr. Trotscha to a chronic care facility at a cost of $1,650 each month — most of which would be paid by the province.

Mrs. Trotscha said she "was put through hell" before the bed was made safe. And then it was not the province, but the March of Dimes which paid the cost. "Here we were saving the taxpayer money by keeping him at home . . . It was as though he weren't dying quickly enough. . . . My husband was so frightened he would be put in a chronic care hospital and I felt I would give him better care at home. It wasn't hard looking after him. I would do it again. The only hard part was fighting people off."

The local administrator agrees with Mrs. Trotscha. Home care should have met the needs of the Trotscha family. But, as an administrator, she was only doing her duty. From the ministry came a more curious response: for two years the ministry has been operating a pilot project in three communities to determine if home care is cheaper than institutional care. The results are due soon. A ministry official volunteered the comment that in a case such as Mr. Trotscha's it probably is cheaper to maintain the patient at home. Beyond that the senior civil servant would not comment. To do so would be to trench upon policy matters. His superior, the minister, was not available for comment.

For reasons of economy alone, government should understand its own best interests: it is far cheaper to allow older people to live outside institutions than to make them wards of the state for the remainder of their lives. To take such a position, however, government would have to give up a most important interest; it would no longer be able to control the aged in quite the same way. Now, government can look at nursing homes or homes for the aged or charitable homes or mental hospitals or any other residential facility and measure effectiveness by bed utilization and cost. To allow the aged to fend for themselves is another matter. How is government to determine whether its dollars are being spent wisely? How is government to know that the old are functioning well with the minimum expenditure of dollars? Guaranteed annual incomes take away the vital element of control from the state and insert in its stead the dynamic of change. None can fully predict what the aged will become nor what the aged will do as a fully functioning part of society.

This is a small risk for the government to take in order to allow the individual the money to remain independent. The potential of a guaranteed income in human terms is beyond measure. It gives to the elderly, and especially older women, for perhaps the first time in their lives the means to stand on their own, the chance not to be dependent.

Money, however, is not an end in itself. The wealthy widow who has been dependent on husband and family for most of her mature life is not made independent by the possession of money alone. She must be taught basic skills for survival; she must learn to fend for herself. This may involve matters as simple as learning to write a cheque or preparing a budget or paying the rent. And these are all matters which are taken from her hands on being admitted to a nursing home.

Beyond financial survival is the need to bring the old into contact with the world around them. For many this may be their first outside contact after having lived most of their lives in the cocoon of the family. The exposure may be frightening; they may be timid; they may prefer isolation to the trauma of encounter and the possibility of rejection. A nursing home allows escape; it permits a sense of aloneness or at the very least a world narrowly defined and tightly structured.

For the state to help place the old in the centre of community life takes more than money. It takes the commitment of people who have imagination, patience, courage and the willingness to measure success in small rather than large steps. It means an end to constructing larger and more remote high-rise senior citizen housing which serves the convenience of staff but only has the effect of taking the old and placing them in an institution which is a nursing home or home for the aged in all but name.

What may be required is scattered housing and apartments in centrally located projects, where the old can live not only with their peers but also among the young.

The old could also live in communes where each would have an apartment, and yet be able to come together for meals or socials. The need for individual space coupled with the opportunity for sharing, for learning to make and keep friends again is important. Out of such an environment can come the kind of love of which Dr. Dave spoke. To this environment must come the support services of the state. The doctor, the rabbi or the minister, the nurse, transportation, and social workers, all would come to the elderly as they live at home in the community. They would visit the apartments of the old and, as guests, do what they can to help. The old would not come to them and be slotted into a position for servicing.

The old need all the love and help they can receive if the final years are to be lived fully. Those years are not always times of joy. Very often they are times of struggle and pain.

It takes strength of body and spirit to turn the final years from despair. There are examples enough to illustrate that the goal can be achieved. In old age Walt Whitman and Tolstoy survived more than one stroke that crippled their bodies and, for a brief time, affected their minds. Both recovered and were highly productive until the end of their lives. But both had reputation, love, others, a habit of working, and a drive to create. In a very real sense they had conditioned themselves early in life to cope with old age.

A zest for life, however, does not mean turning away from the reality of life, which includes death. Nor does it mean the false perpetuation of youth. A sense of individual control is implicit; that is, the zest for life must accept what life implies: joy, sorrow, happiness and pain. Such acceptance brings personal well-being, personal health. The medical profession can enhance personal health; its machines and technology can never provide an adequate substitute for emotional and spiritual health.

Ivan Illich writes:

> A world of optimal and widespread health is obviously a world of minimal and only occasional medical intervention. Healthy people are those who live in healthy homes on a healthy diet in an environment equally fit for birth, growth, work, healing, and dying; they are sustained by a culture that enhances the conscious acceptance of limits to population, of aging, of incomplete recovery and ever-imminent death. Healthy people need minimal bureaucratic interference to mate, give birth, share the human condition, and die.
>
> Man's consciously lived fragility, individuality, and relatedness make the experience of pain, of sickness, and of death an integral part of his life. The ability to cope with this trio autonomously is fundamental to his health. As he becomes dependent on the management of his intimacy, he renounces his autonomy and his health must decline. The true miracle of modern medicine is diabolical. It consists in making not only individuals but whole populations survive on inhumanly low levels of personal health. Medical nemesis is the negative feedback of a social organization that set out to improve and equalize the opportunity for each man to cope in autonomy and ended by destroying it [*Limits to Medicine: Medical Nemesis* . . . (1969)].

For society, the challenge is not to abandon the elderly, but to embrace them. The widow who was daughter, wife and mother can sit alone in an institution; she can be well fed, cared for medically, and given necessary physical exercises. All this is not enough. There is a further goal; the need in the final years to encourage her to live, not to be warehoused for death.

EPILOGUE

The aged are denied the right to work. They are discriminated against in employment, and the law implicitly encourages their forced retirement.

Society saps old people's will to remain independent. Excluded from the work force and condemned to a fixed income, they grow more frail as inflation makes their dollars worth less. How much easier it must seem to yield themselves to the state, to let the state care for them, to give up the fight for survival as individuals.

Some survive and are strong and active in old age. Yet for many the surrender is formal and final. The aged declare of their own free will that they are no longer able to care for themselves; their health is fragile and can be maintained only with the help of the province. And the province, for its part, after due consideration, will accept them.

For the man who spent his life working the surrender is hard. For so many years he was productive. Every day, five days a week, eight hours a day he went to work with others. He was paid a salary or a commission, and he understood well how success was measured. Now he enters a world of full-time leisure. What is he to do between meals, baths and television except sleep?

For the widow who spent her life as wife and mother the surrender is hard. She must accept the fact that her husband is gone and her children removed. She has only her scrapbook, her book of photos and her memories. She, more than the man, will use her leisure time to talk with others of the past and of the present where she has no control, no real opportunity to be useful. She can neither cook, nor clean, nor care for others. She is there to be cared for.

Good health is a state of mind and heart as well as body. The most damaging blow to the good health of the aged is to exclude them from the mainstream of the community by removing them to institutions where the environment is sterile. All too often care is administered by uniformed attendants who treat the aged as if they were infants. In such a setting what strength it must take for the mind to remain alert and the body active and alive. How difficult it must be for the aged to see themselves as mature adults leading a full life when they are so totally segregated:

    —They cannot have the company of the greater community. They are largely confined to a life with other institutionalized persons and their keepers.

—They do not have a sense of their own territory, their own space which they can control and make into a home. At best, they live two to a room separated by a wall divider. Except for a few pictures and some small treasures the room is furnished and maintained by the institution.

—They are denied the opportunity for sexual congress. Males are separated from females. Doors cannot be locked. In the name of good health care, of checkups, intrusions into the lives of residents are the rule.

—They can neither select nor prepare their own food. They must eat the "nutritiously balanced meals" given. And they must eat these meals in a common room.

—They cannot care for themselves. Their rooms are tidied by a staff. Even their very persons are tended by the home staff.

In many respects the institutionalized aged are removed from the community and carefully isolated, packaged, and warehoused for death. This state of affairs need not continue.

The central goal of any community should be to help its members become and remain fully productive. This must not only benefit the individual, but also the community. With regard to the aged, there is no magic in determining how that goal should be achieved: because institutions can kill, they should be places of last resort. Emphasis should be placed on home care, on the support services which will allow the aged to live at home as long as possible. This, in turn, means reorganizing methods for providing home care services to suit the needs of the aged rather than the convenience of programme administrators.

Stress on home care means a reordering of priorities. Today government funds are directed toward subsidizing the costs of hospital care and physicians' bills. The expense is enormous and it is accelerating rapidly. In many respects, the regulatory scheme controlling institutions housing the aged can be seen as a way of reducing hospital and physician expense: it is much cheaper to keep older persons in nursing homes than chronic care hospital wards. And government, to some extent, can control the "medical subsidy" to nursing homes. Under the broad heading of "extended care," government can defend the services for which it will pay as well as the amount of payment.

To speak of home care is to move far from subsidizing hospital and physician care. The full support of home care may have no direct or immediate effect on hospital or medical costs. Our concern is not the treatment or cure of a particular illness. Our concern is not providing incidental home support until there is full recovery from surgery. Our concern, rather, is to encourage and assist the aged to retain and enrich their lives in the community.

The home support of which we write requires a budget and an infrastructure unrelated to the *existing* medical care programme. And the support of which we speak will cost money. It is not good enough to rely on volunteers operating from hundreds of well-meaning charities to provide meals-on-wheels, or visiting nurses or homemakers. The aged should have a full range of services readily available whether they live in cities, or towns or the country. Most important, these services should be offered as a matter of right, not as an act of charity. The aged should be reinforced in their sense of self-worth.

Home care is just a beginning. There is a need to assist the aged in remaining and, in many instances, for the first time coming into the community mainstream. Creative living and senior citizen centres are desirable. Through arts and handicrafts the aged can be encouraged to communicate. More often than not, however, that communication is by and between the aged themselves, and not with others. The challenge is to find and help to stimulate the talent, the experience and the imagination of the aged in the interest of themselves — and the entire community.

The aged can work for the benefit of all. They could have so many opportunities. Why can't the aged assist in the operation of day care centres? Why can't the aged help in the education and rehabilitation of the retarded? Why can't the aged be called upon to relate the oral histories which they alone carry, and which on their death will be lost forever — unless the young are wise enough to ask and listen?

To change policy requires will. The aged have the vote, but they form no powerful lobby. This need not always remain so. There may come a day when the aged will recognize that they are a large group with interests in common. Pensioners Concerned, a lobbying organization for the aged, already is making efforts in this direction.

Government has established the trappings for so-called senior citizen policy input. There are government advisory panels, and with regularity the panels submit reports which, more often than not, are filed, as government goes about the business of managing the collection and distribution of tax dollars.

Until the aged are ready to speak for themselves the community at large must question and speak on their behalf. If citizens are concerned about the use of tax moneys, they might well question whether those moneys are spent on medical care for the aged or if they are used primarily to warehouse the aged? The answer seems clear: nearly all of those who enter institutions never leave until they die. If medical care means rehabilitation of the aged, the record of achievement is dismal indeed.

There are questions that go beyond the use of tax dollars: Why has the community chosen to isolate its aged members? What needs are satisfied by the institution of nursing homes? Why haven't home care services developed as in other nations?

The questions and the answers will cause discomfort not only to the young but also to the aged. The isolation of the aged is no accident. It is a conscious act. It is done because the larger community does not want to see and does not want to cope with the aged. The old do not have the face of youth. The old look upon their own mortality, and their faces mirror what every human being must encounter. In our society, however, death is denied. It is not accepted as a part of life.

The aged often allow themselves to be treated as a class of untouchables. If the larger community shuns them, then the aged may shun themselves. In no small measure, the aged allow themselves to be moved into institutions where the doors will forever close behind them. Too often the aged do not rail against a system that would deny life. Too often they are passive; they go gently into that dark night; they do not shout against the storm of inhumanity.

For the young and the old there is a challenge posed by two questions. It is a simple challenge, and on their answer will depend the shape of public policy: Will the young and the old choose life? Will the young and the old accept the fact of death as a part of life and, in that setting, live fully?

NOTES:

NOTES: Chapter One

1. Another Way: Respect for Self

The internationally known visitor referred to in this section is Dr. L.Z. Cousin, Clinical Director, Oxfordshire Area Health Authority (Teaching), The Cowley Road Hospital, Oxford, England. Dr. Cousin's experience is set out in *Proceedings of The Institute on Long-Term Care*, sponsored by the Ontario Hospital Association, the Ontario Association of Homes for the Aged, and the Ontario Nursing Home Association, December 2-3, 1974, OHA Centre, Don Mills, Ontario.

Dr. Cousin accepted the fact that there might be an institutional need to care for elderly, confused, wandering patients. But even here he stressed individual freedom that could be built into the institution:

> Finally I said that if we were going to deal with elderly, confused, wandering patients, then perhaps the basis of the day-hospital might well be giving them an endless corridor round which to wander for 5 or 6 hours a day, without easily getting out at all. They could get to the appropriate sanitary services when they wanted to; they could walk into the dining room when appropriate; they were getting the best sedation, physical activity, (their serum lactic acid was going up quite a bit) and they slept well at home at night without sedatives or tranquillizers. Then we ran into a very interesting snag. The patients accepted this and would wander off happily, never getting anywhere at all, always under supervision and observation, but the professional staff, with their feelings of anxiety and guilt, when they saw an old man vigorously stride down the corridor, would try to rush after him and restrain him. It became very difficult to impress them that if they only walked in the opposite direction, they would do far better. And even this failed so that really, one had to instruct the nurses on duty, not so much the occupational therapists, that really all they had to do when he started rushing down the corridor was to take out a cigarette. They should light it and take three puffs by which time they would realize they were walking in the opposite direction and meet him, perhaps at the first corner. If they were still very worried then we prescribed six puffs on the cigarette and they would meet him about the second corner. If they were terribly disturbed then they should smoke the whole cigarette and they would meet him back from where he started. This is an

example of this interface again, of anxiety and guilt and worry; understandably worry and guilt in case the staff should be blamed for some sort of accident that might take place'' [*Proceedings*, pp. 54-55].

2. The Canadian Way: More Institutions

There is some difficulty, because of definitional problems, in arriving at a consensus of how many nursing home beds are available for Canada's elderly population. The Table on page 124 sets out four estimates of the number of nursing homes, homes for the aged and related institutions.

Nursing homes are defined under the Canada Assistance Plan Regulations as ''a home for any age group where nursing is provided,'' whereas homes for the aged are defined as ''residential institutions for domiciliary, supervisory, personal or nursing care for persons aged 60 and over.'' In other words, the two terms are not mutually exclusive and may in fact be synonymous. The levels of care that may be provided in the institutions are defined as domiciliary, supervisory, personal, nursing and social rehabilitation but any combination of these levels of care may exist in any one home.

A Canada-wide view of home care as well as hospital services is contained in ''Implications of The Changing Age Structure of the Canadian Population,'' *Study on Population and Technology, Perceptions 2*, Science Council of Canada (Ottawa: 1976), pp. 46-48. At pp. 47-48 the report stated:

Home care for the elderly has been discussed thus far primarily as a form of health service. In addition to supplementing medical care, home help and other supportive services must be viewed as the primary means of maintaining the independence of elderly citizens and of preventing, or at least postponing, institutionalization. Most home care services in Canada are still mainly concerned with caring for those who have been released from hospital. This is very different from assisting elderly persons over an extended period in daily chores so they may maintain their independence.

Nevertheless, there are numerous supportive programs in Canada which can assist the elderly in remaining in their own homes. Many cities are experimenting with or have, in fact, established such services as Meals-on Wheels, Dial-a-Friend, day care centres, and ''friendly visiting''. In Winnipeg, for example, day care centres are now operating at two nursing homes. Elderly persons are brought to the centre one day a week, in the initial stages of the program, and are able to participate in social and

Number of Nursing Homes, Homes for the Aged and Related Institutions, Canada 1973

Province	Canada Assistance Plan Directorate[1]		Canada Assistance Plan Directorate[2]		Canadian Hospital Association[3]		Statistics Canada Hospital Division[4]	
	No.	Beds	No.	Beds	No.	Beds	No.	Beds
British Columbia	493	11,782	493	11,590	61	3,240	59	2,934
Alberta	137	9,162	140	9,242	173	10,962	103	8,384
Saskatchewan	105	6,212	105	6,071	112	6,816	112	6,755
Manitoba	86	5,662	87	5,680	89	6,675	96	6,881
Ontario	621	46,365	644	46,631	627	48,112	628	50,132
Quebec	443	24,061	448	24,190	407	22,875	614	38,660
New Brunswick	84	2,724	84	2,710	77	2,588	77	2,952
Nova Scotia	132	5,086	133	5,271	55	3,698	57	3,668
Prince Edward Island	11	1,022	11	1,057	15	1,170	16	1,013
Newfoundland	33	1,234	32	1,220	16	1,206	11	713
Northwest Territories	3	77	—	—	3	30	2	20
Yukon	—	—	4	89	1	15	1	5
Canada	2,148	113,387	2,182	113,851	1,636	107,387	1,776	122,127

Sources: [1] "Statistical Information on Homes for Special Care, March 31, 1973," *Program Information and Evaluation.* Department of National Health and Welfare, Ottawa, January 1974.

[2] Homes for Special Care listed in the C.A.P. Agreement Schedule "A" up to 31.3.73. Income Support Division, Department of National Health and Welfare, Ottawa, December 1973.

[3] "Summary of Nursing Homes and Related Institutions," *Canadian Hospital Directory.* Canadian Hospital Association, July 1973.

[4] "Summary of Related Institutions in Canada 1974," *List of Canadian Hospitals and Related Institutions and Facilities 1974.* Statistics Canada, February 1974.

recreational activities. . . . In addition, routine health maintenance and examination is possible: supervision of medication,
checking of blood pressure. Over 200 of Winnipeg's elderly are
also visited by volunteers as part of the Friendly Visiting Service
sponsored by the Age and Opportunity Centre.

While such programs are becoming more common throughout
Canada, most are very limited in scope, relying primarily on
volunteers and insufficient funding from a variety of private and
public sources. In Toronto, for instance, over half of the supportive service for the elderly is provided by church groups and other
informal volunteer organizations. This can be a very positive
factor, in that it evokes personal involvement and dedication, but
it may also hamper the coordination of efforts and the overall
effectiveness of programs. The elderly in one community may be
inundated with meals, visits, telephone checks and recreational
activities, while those in another part of town–often those of more
limited means — must fend for themselves.

There is a clear need now to plan for more thorough coordination of such services, if choice and accessibility are important
social goals.

3. For specific categories of diagnosis, the increases in patient days are
even more dramatic. For example, in 1971, those over 65 accounted for
80.3 per cent of all the hospitalization in general and allied special
hospitals due to cerebrovascular diseases. By 2001 this percentage will
have increased to 84.5 per cent. The Long Range Health Planning
Report warned that in planning for the future

It will be necessary to take significant steps towards the provision
of more or different hospital facilities for persons 65 and over,
while simultaneously reducing the rate of hospital occupancy for
this same group of people. If no steps are taken in these directions
and hospital utilization patterns remain about the same as they are
now, and the provision of hospital beds continues at current rates,
there will be an increase of 28.2 million in the number of patient
days in general and allied hospitals.

Of more significance, however, is where this increase will be
concentrated. 15.1 million patient days, or more than half of the
anticipated increase, will be attributable to persons 65 and over.
Of these 15.1 million patient days, 6.1 million will be due to
normal population growth and 9 million will be due to the increasing proportion of the aged in the population.

The cost will likely be more than this society can bear. To provide for an additional 15 million days will require about 150 three hundred-bed hospitals operating at 100 per cent occupancy. *The cost for each bed of such a hospital is estimated at $40,000.*

4. Excluded from Life

Much of the information in this section is found in D. Baum, *The Final Plateau: The Betrayal of Our Older Citizens* (Toronto: Burns & MacEachern, 1974). It is instructive to note a different projection. See "Population, Technology and Resources," Science Council of Canada, Report No. 25 (Ottawa: 1976), p.11. (It must be emphasized, however, that the Science Council is offering a projection for the 1980s.)

> There is plenty of work to be done, and very little involuntary unemployment. During the 1980's when growth of the labour force began to slow down while development increased, it seemed that Canada would need to attract huge numbers of immigrants. However, working conditions were improved, and means were found to reverse the labour growth decline through the participation in the work force of more women, young and retired people, and we were able to meet these labour needs from Canadian sources. The leisure revolution turned out to be an illusion; leisure hours are no more numerous than they were in the 1970's. We simply know how to use them better, and more attention is paid to recreational facilities — which are becoming accessible to larger and larger numbers of people.
>
> Most manpower economists' projections proved inaccurate. Rather than each year's additions to the labour force being destined solely for service occupations, it has turned out that we need unexpectedly large numbers of skilled professionals and tradespeople in the food and other resource sectors. For a brief period, the universities and colleges were unprepared for the sudden demand for agronomists, hydrologists, geochemists, and engineers of all kinds. There were also brief shortages of skilled tradespeople such as pipe fitters and sheet metal workers.
>
> There are good numbers of well-educated and committed young people, but the population is generally older, although healthy. The emphasis on preventive health care, rather than on treating sickness, is beginning to pay off. There is an increasing proportion of seventy- and eighty-year-olds, who, because of flexible retirement policies and other measures, actively contribute to the community, rather than depend on institutional care.

The population continues to grow, but slowly, and will stabilize within a generation. At the beginning of the twenty first century, the pessimism and foreboding of the 1970's looks old-fashioned, and Canadians feel that the future looks manageable.
This is a view — but a realizable one. It depends on three crucial factors. First, we must adopt and maintain a slower population growth than Canada knew in the last quarter century; a population of 29 rather than 35 million in the year 2001 would increase our options substantially. Second, we need to have available the skills and knowledge to implement all the technologies on which our preferred future depends. Finally, there has to be an informed public consensus to proceed in this direction. The decision has to be made.

As to materials concerned with housing the elderly, see *Mayor's Task Force Report on The Disabled and Elderly* (Toronto: 1974), pp. 10-12; D. Bairstow, "Demographic and Economic Aspects of Housing Canada's Elderly," Central Mortgage and Housing Corporation (CMHC) Policy Planning Diversion (Ottawa: 1973); *Housing The Elderly*, CMHC (Ottawa: 1975), revised edition.

5. Basic Needs: At Home Care

Again, the stories concerning England come from Dr. Cousin, see Note 1. See also N. Markus, "Home Care for the Aged," 12, *On Growing Old* (1973), pp. 1-8; C.W. Schwenger, "Keep the Old Folks at Home," 65, *Canadian Journal of Public Health*, 417 (1974).

The Science Council of Canada, referring to a *United Nations Report of the Secretary-General*, "Question of The Elderly and The Aged," United Nations (New York; 1973), stated on p. 107:

Why the extraordinary differences between Great Britain and Canada? Such things as climate, geography, population mobility and family relationships are important. Undoubtedly, however, one of the main factors is that in Canada home care services were not insured simultaneously with hospital and institutional care (as was done in Great Britain under the National Health Service). As a result, continuous pressure has existed for years in this country to place far too many sick and frail older people in institutions. In addition, Great Britain has not had the money to put into expensive buildings, and has had to "make do" with the relatively less expensive alternative of looking after a much higher proportion of the elderly in a home setting. This has proven to be a boon to many elderly who would much rather be looked after at home if it is at all possible and if given a real alternative. The desire of the elderly to maintain their independence appears to be a widely accepted fact, yet, as the United Nations report indicates:

"In this connection, an example of national policies is the all too frequent high priority given to long-term institutional care and facilities for the aged. This is particularly so in many of the developed countries and a trend in this direction is appearing in developing countries. There is and will continue to be a need for such facilities for the elderly. However, for many older persons, such institutionalization should not be the place of first resort in meeting their social and health-care needs. Only recently has this practice of institutionalization of the aged been called into question and the view is increasingly expressed that a full range of community alternatives including community-based and coordinated home care services should be provided through an explicit policy of keeping persons in their own homes as long as possible through the development of supportive community resources and services" [pp. 59-60].

NOTES: Chapter Two

1. Goals and Results

The story of Mrs. Schramm, like every other story in this book, is real. It has been told to dramatize the effects of institutionalization. The same story can be told by many others as *The Toronto Star* discovered. See B. Zosky, "Don't Put Me in a Home — Woman 85," *The Toronto Star*, February 19, 1977, p. 1, A. 12. To carry forward the tale of institutionalization without reason one additional story will be retold of the several presented by *The Toronto Star*.

Mrs. Gertrude Green, a widow, is 85. She asks: "Don't put me in an old folks' home . . . I'd get claustrophobic and die there. And I'm not ready to die yet." In 1976 Mrs. Green, "a witty, vivacious and irrepressible 85-year-old, decided that nothing would ever get her into any kind of senior citizens' residence." Her five daughters advised her to give up her Oriole Road apartment and all her furnishings, and move to a pleasant private senior residence at their expense. "I got angry," she says. "And I told them before I'd ever agree, I'd find myself a little room in a hotel somewhere and they'd never find me."

Her family had been paying the rent. At that point Mrs. Green decided it was time to stop accepting financial help from her children and live entirely on her government pensions, Old Age Security and Guaranteed Annual Income Supplement (GAINS). The federal Old Age Security pays individuals $141.34 a month and the provincial GAINS programme, applied in combination with the federal Guaranteed Income Supplement, ensures that an individual has an annual income of $3,352.

Mrs. Green applied for government-subsidized housing. There would be no institutional life for her. "When you get old, people just want you to sit in a corner. But this is one person who is not going to." Mrs. Green says she's convinced that people who go into institutions "start to get senile fast. Besides, at 85 I've earned the right to do what I want to do. . . . And I don't want to live in a place where people are continuously knocking on my door telling me when to eat and when to sleep. . . . I got my family through the depression and World War II, and if I want to sit around all day in my night gown or watch a late movie 'till two in the morning, that's what I'm going to do . . . I don't like people pestering me."

John MacKay, president of Extendicare Ltd. (see page 22), and chairman of the board of Community Care Services, a social service agency, is sympathetic to Mrs. Green's point of view:

We know the trauma to individuals admitted to a nursing home. They are used to their own home where they have privacy. All of a sudden they are thrust in with hundreds of people. . . . When they go to eat, for example, they eat in a large dining room. I know I enjoy eating at a banquet sometimes, but I like a quiet corner sometimes too. . . . The public doesn't realize the suffering and hardship of people living in fear on a fixed income.

If they can't make it on their own "there is only one place they can go [a nursing home] and that's not a very happy thought."

The story of Mrs. Green was not over once she applied for subsidized housing. It did not even end once the application was accepted. The offered apartment was isolated: five blocks from the nearest store and an enormous distance from her friends. Her arthritis would not permit subway transportation; she simply could not manage the steep steps to and from the subway. "I realize I should be grateful for the government's help, and I am. . . . But I couldn't manage living like that."

She sought and obtained help from Canadian Pensioners Concerned. Government found that it could be more accomodating. Mrs. Green is located in the downtown area, close to her friends and shopping. She is in an apartment furnished with her belongings. And she is managing quite well on her Old Age Security and GAINS cheques.

Government's approach to subsidized housing as contrasted to institutional housing is simply incomprehensible. Government will provide a subsidy for persons such as Mrs. Green only after much argument. On the other hand, government has increased the number of senior citizen "homes," institutional structures, almost without restraint. Ontario in December 1974 had 26,300 senior citizen residence beds — as many as the nursing home industry in the province. For each senior citizen bed the province paid 80 per cent of the cost up to *$13.50 a day*. If the resident is unable to pay the remaining $5.45, the province pays 80 per cent of that portion (extended care, see Chapter 3). For residential care the province also pays a large percentage of the daily rate.

By legislation, all cities, counties, municipalities and districts with more than 15,000 population, and Indian Bands are required to establish homes for senior citizens. Yet there are few prescribed legislative or administrative standards for such homes which more and more are offering extended care service. This lack of standards, for example, applies to admission policies.

The occupancy rate for senior citizen housing is about 90%.

Government itself stressed the incongruity of senior citizen housing as contrasted to home care support. See *Report of the Ontario Inter-*

ministerial Committee on Residential Services to the Cabinet Committee on Social Development (Toronto: Queen's Printer), 1975, p. 86:

> Although there are many services for senior citizens in their own homes as alternatives to institutional and satellite home care, these have been slow to develop in Ontario relative to the size of the population. Examples are meals-on-wheels, day care, short-term care (vocation care), elderly persons centres, transportation, etc. These services are often given by the homes themselves. The experience of other Provinces and countries suggests that we in Ontario tend to provide strong financial and other incentives for the elderly to go into institutions rather than remain in the community with the aid of support services. A person in a senior citizens home is provided with a $43 comfort allowance at least (higher if on Extended Care) if on OAS-GIS-GAINS. This amount of discretionary income would not be feasible if a person receiving the same benefits lived in the community in unsubsidized accomodation.

2. Flexible Housing

See *Housing The Elderly*, Central Mortgage and Housing Corporation (Ottawa: 1975). At p.7 the report warns of high density construction in terms of the elderly:

> Many elderly support a concept of housing projects built exclusively for the use of senior citizens. This outlook may stem from a sense of being at ease within their own age group, and relating their pace of activities to contemporaries. Economies derived from high-density construction are also tending to increase the number of units built in one location. The results are growing concentrations of elderly people in small areas creating possibilities of overtaxing social, recreation and health services in the community. . . . It is becoming increasingly important to examine, within the planning process, the physical and social impact of large senior citizens' projects on existing neighborhoods. Surveys should explore not only current capabilities of facilities and services, but also the projected demand for housing by the elderly and its probable impact on community resources. . . . There is evidence to indicate that the quality and efficiency of administrative services within a project are dependent upon the project size. More facilities can be provided and staffs utilized more efficiently in projects of 150 to 200 units than in smaller projects. Beyond this point, however, gains in efficiency are not significant. There is also a danger that in larger projects the face-to-face contact between staff and residents may be replaced by a more impersonal bureaucratic relationship.

Let there be no doubt that institutionalization, and certainly premature institutionalization, can kill. So, too, can a change from one institutional environment to another. As to both points see G. Downey, "Must a Transfer Order be a Death Sentence for SNF Patients," *Modern Health Care* (October 1974), p. 44; E. Ogren and M. Linn, "Male Nursing Home Patients: Relocation and Mortality," 19, *Journal of The American Geriatrics Society*, 229 (1971); E. Killian, "Effect of Geriatric Transfers on Mortality Rates," *Social Work* (January 1970), p. 19; V. Prock, "Effects of Institutionalization: A Comparison of Community, Waiting List, and Institutionalized Aged Persons," 59, *American Journal of Public Health* (1969), 1837; C. Aldrich and E. Mendkoff, "Relocation of the Aged and Disabled: A Mortality Study," 11, *Journal of The American Geriatrics Society* (1963), 185.

3. Bigger Institutions

The description of Baycrest Geriatric Centre comes largely, but not exclusively, from the excellent doctoral thesis of Professor Judith S. Posner, Atkinson College, York University, entitled: "Perceptions of Physical and Mental Incompetence in a Home for the Aged" (York University, 1975). In addition, however, we had the benefit of the experience of Ms. Linda Grobovsky, formerly a social worker with Jewish Family Service of Toronto. As a social worker Ms. Grobovsky had many in-depth contacts with Baycrest, its staff and its residents.

The book *Consider Yourself at Home* (Toronto: Department of Social and Family Services, 1971) consists of 111 pages. Not a single page focuses upon the living quarters, as such, of the residents. Not a single page contains a picture of their bedrooms. The book does consist almost entirely of pictures, large and glossy, of the exterior of each home for the aged.

4. A "Model" Nursing Home

The "model" nursing home is based on a description and evaluation by R. Skerman, a psychiatric social worker at the Scarborough Centenary Hospital in Metropolitan Toronto. See R. Skerman, "Bringing the 'Quality of Life' to Nursing Home Residents," *Hospital Administration in Canada* (July 1976), p. 30. As noted, the facility described is operated by Extendicare Ltd., a public company, whose president reported to shareholders that consolidated revenue in 1975 was $48,959,371 compared with $34,340,019 for the previous twelve-month period. Net earnings from continuing operations were $1,900,553, or 95.5 cents per share, up from fiscal 1974 net earnings of $1,318,028, or 79.6 cents per share (*Annual Report, Extendicare Ltd.*, 1975, p. 2).

See *Building Better*, A Survey of Ontario Homes for the Aged as Received by Residents and by an Independent Group of Senior Citizens (Toronto: Associated Senior Executives of Canada Ltd., 1974). In its conclusion the survey states:

The design and equipment of Homes for the Aged in Ontario has undergone some major changes for the better in recent years. This survey included homes in buildings more than 50 years old and some which first opened their doors in 1973. The advances in building techniques and material were obvious. It was equally clear that architects were applying much more imagination to their designs and creating handsome buildings. It is important that these Homes be attractive and welcoming to the public and, particularly, to the senior citizens of the community. Care should be exercised however to ensure that interior design and equipment needed for the comfort and convenience of residents is not sacrificed for the sake of an imposing exterior.

Many of the short-comings commented on in the foregoing pages seem to stem from failure to appreciate the numbers of residents who have physical handicaps impairing their mobility. Twenty-five percent of the 599 interviewed for this study were dependent on wheel chairs, crutches or canes. To this number should be added a further group who have less than full use of their arms or hands. It is clear therefore that building design and equipment must accommodate themselves to the needs of this group. Over and above this particular problem of mobility it must be recognized that advancing years take a toll of general physical strength, agility and sight. The design, equipment and furnishing objectives must be to make it as easy as possible for all residents to move about and live comfortably and independently.

Major Recommendations
In summary, the major recommendations are as follows:
1. Smaller Homes — an optimum size of 150 to 200 beds.
2. Single Storey Buildings rather than multi-storey, with a principal objective of eliminating elevators.
3. Automatic Doors and safer ramps for all building entrances and exits.
4. The majority of residents' rooms should be 2-bed rooms but there is a need for more single rooms and for more married couple accommodation. Four-bed rooms should be retained only for residents who need extensive bed care from the nursing staff.
5. More toilet, washing and bathing facilities, more conveniently located, are a pressing need.
6. Maximum integration of the Home and its residents with the community should be a prime objective.

Many other suggestions have been made, most of them easily incorporated in some existing Homes as well as in Homes to be built. However, if the above six concepts guide the planning of new Homes a great step forward will have been taken towards better accommodation for Senior Citizens.

Finally, we recommend that similar surveys to this one should be made at intervals of no more than five years, in order that planning and building guidelines remain current.

See also *This Is My Life and This Is My Home*, Survey of Regional Municipality of Niagara Homes for Senior Citizens, Residents Councils of the Niagara Region Homes for Senior Citizens (1974). The survey dealt with residents of both homes for the aged (HA) and nursing homes (NH). As to bedrooms, the survey stated at p. 26:

In NH there were two important complaints. First, a lack of privacy in the bedrooms. *There was an almost total absence of privacy curtains in the NH. All residents dressed and undressed in view of each other.* Most of the HA have privacy curtains, which provide a great deal of satisfaction to the residents. Second, the residents complained about a *lack of cupboard space in the bedrooms for their possessions.* Some residents commented that their clothes were placed among several cupboards in different bedrooms. This resulted in some residents, who normally would be able to dress themselves, [being] dependent on the staff to bring them their clothes. In HA and NH there again seems to be a lack of bedroom facilities to meet the needs of wheelchair residents. Most of the non-ambulatory residents stated that the *cupboards were too high and [they needed assistance to reach their possessions.* It is interesting to note that one-third of this group stated that *if they* could reach the articles themselves they could be more independent, and rely less on the staff to do simple tasks for them.

NOTES: Chapter Three

1. A Seller's Market: Standards for Admission

It is instructive to view the information given to the public as contrasted to information actually required of applicants in homes for the aged. Toronto, a wealthy city, was selected for this purpose. What follows is first a brochure describing admission standards for a municipal-run home for the aged, and, second, on pages 137-9 the actual form transferring assets. (These materials are based on 1974 requirements.)

Our Residences

So that Senior Citizens, sixty years of age and over, who are no longer able to adequately care for themselves in the Community, may continue their accustomed life style wherever and whenever possible, Residences, provided by the Municipality of Metropolitan Toronto through The Ontario Homes for the Aged and Rest Homes Act, are available to help meet their needs when community based supportive services can no longer do so alone.

Personal Care is available for Residents requiring a minimum of assistance such as getting in and out of bed, with bathing and some nursing or medical care as well as for those who are not eligible for admission to a Hospital (Active, Convalescent or Chronic Care) but do need, among other things considerable nursing care. Specialized Care is also offered for those Residents who may have disabilities related to the aging process requiring more supervision and assistance because of mild mental disability, confusion or disorientation.

What Will It Cost?

The cost of maintenance which includes necessary drugs or medications is based on the actual cost of the Residences' operation and may be adjusted annually. The present rate is $20.75 per day. If financially able, a Resident pays the daily rate but if unable to do so the Resident receives $43 from his monthly income and the balance is applied towards the actual cost. Unpaid maintenance is recoverable from his assets if the Resident's circumstances change and are claimable from his estate. To establish financial ability, a confidential review of income and assets is necessary; it is suggested that you discuss your maintenance payments at that time. But whatever the amount paid, a Resident receives all the services provided by the Residence which are necessary. An Extended Care Programme Application is made for all Residents who are not already approved as eligible at the time of admission. If granted Extended Care Benefits the Resident pays $6.15 per day and the balance of the maintenance cost is paid by the Extended Care Programme and the Metropolitan Corporation.

How To Apply

Applications for admission are made through the Home Admissions Unit, 350 Christie Street, Toronto, M6G 3C3 (Telephone 367-8631).

You may apply to come and live with us if you are over the age of sixty or if you are under sixty when there are special circumstances that prevent your being cared for properly elsewhere. There are certain medical conditions that cannot be looked after in the Residences, our Medical Advisory Board examines all applications to ensure that we would be able to care for you properly. If you have any doubt about your own medical eligibility, please call the Home Admissions Unit (367-8631).

2. The Meaning of Admission: Unspoken Fears

The Ontario standards concerning admission are about as rigorous as any jurisdiction in North America. The relevant legislation is contained in Homes for the Aged and Rest Homes Act, Revised Statutes of Ontario 1970, as amended, Chapter 206, and The Nursing Homes Act, Statutes of Ontario 1972, as amended, Chapter 11.

Homes for the Aged may admit any person:
(a) who is over the age of sixty years and incapable of supporting himself or unable to care properly for himself;
(b) who is over sixty and mentally incompetent and who requires care, supervision and control for his protection, but who is not suitable for a psychiatric facility under the Mental Health Act;
(c) who is over sixty and who requires bed care and general personal nursing services, but does not require care in a hospital; or
(d) who is under the age of sixty and who because of special circumstances cannot be cared for adequately elsewhere (if approval of the minister is obtained.)

Section 18 of the 1972 act providing for committal by a provincial judge was repealed but there is no provision, as there is in the Ontario regulations, that a resident may only be admitted with his consent or the consent of his next of kin or legal representative.

THE MUNICIPALITY OF METROPOLITAN TORONTO
DEPARTMENT OF SOCIAL SERVICES
Homes for the Aged

TO THE MUNICIPALITY OF METROPOLITAN TORONTO, HEREIN REFERRED TO AS "THE METROPOLITAN CORPORATION".

I, _____, having applied for admission to a Home for the Aged of the Metropolitan Corporation, in consideration of the benefits now or hereafter given to me, do hereby:

1.   Agree to pay the Metropolitan Corporation, insofar as I am able, for my maintenance at prevailing rates in any Home for the Aged maintained by the said Metropolitan Corporation in which I have lived or may hereafter live.

2.   Transfer and assign to the Metropolitan Corporation, all payments of pension hereafter due to me or any income hereafter received by me to apply such sum as the Metropolitan Corporation may deem proper toward payment of my maintenance as aforesaid and to return the balance to me.

3.   Authorize the Metropolitan Corporation or any duly authorized representative of the Department of Social Services thereof, to examine any account held by me or in which I have any interest in any Chartered Bank or other financial institution and authorize any such Chartered Bank or other Financial Institution to disclose all information which it may have with regard to any such account or to any assets belonging to me.

4.   Agree with the Metropolitan Corporation to transfer and deposit all cash, stocks, bonds and all other liquid assets of any kind, which I have on hand or in any such Bank or Financial Institution to and in a personal trust fund in the said Home for the Aged.

5.   Give to the Commissioner of Social Services of the Metropolitan Corporation and his successors from time to time full power and authority to sell, call in and convert into money, in his or their sole discretion, all the said stocks, bonds and other liquid assets of any kind referred to in Item 4 hereof and pay into my said Trust Fund the proceeds thereof; and to hereby exonerate the said Commissioner and his successors from time to time and the Metropolitan Corporation or any of them from any responsibility for loss or damage which may be occasioned by any such sale, calling in, or conversion made or carried out in good faith.

6. Agree with the Metropolitan Corporation that it may charge monthly to my said Trust Fund the full cost of my maintenance at prevailing rates applicable to the said Home (less any amounts applied to such maintenance pursuant to Item 2) until my account has been reduced to a balance of $500.00, such amount to be held in Trust for me to provide for personal expenditures and funeral expenses as approved by the Commissioner of Social Services and no further charges to be made thereupon unless I leave the said Home in which event any balance outstanding for my maintenance shall forthwith become due and payable and may be deducted from any balance in my Trust Fund, or realized by the sale of any assets held in trust for me by the Commissioner of the Metropolitan Corporation, which sale may be made without my consent and will be upon such terms as the Commissioner shall consider to be in the best interests of the Metropolitan Corporation.

7. Agree with the Metropolitan Corporation that I will enter into and execute any deed or other instrument deemed necessary by the solicitor for the Metropolitan Corporation to constitute myself a trustee for the said Corporation of any interest which I now have or may hereafter be entitled to in any land, such interest to be held by me in trust as security for the payment of my maintenance at prevailing rates as before mentioned and to be charged to the extent of such maintenance costs not otherwise paid by me hereunder.

8. Agree upon my decease that after funeral expenses have been paid all remaining monies or assets to my credit in Residents of Homes for the Aged Trust Account, shall be applied firstly against all maintenance charges owing to any municipality of Metropolitan Toronto Home for the Aged.

9. Certify that the following is a complete list of all the property and income which I now own or to which I am now entitled, together with a list of all assets which have been transferred during the past by me to any other person or persons.

NOTE: Each Section must be answered. Where there are no assets or income, answer "Nil".

1. CASH in my possession $ _____

2. BANK ACCOUNTS

Bank	Branch	Account No.	$

3. PENSIONS
   & ANNUITIES   OAS ; $ OAA ; $

Other _____

4. LIFE INSURANCE
   Company   No.   Face   Beneficiary   Location

5. REAL ESTATE
   Address   Encumbrance   Rental Income

6. INVESTMENTS — BONDS (B): STOCKS (S): MORTGAGE
   RECEIVABLE (M).
   Type (B.S. or M.)   Debtor or Company   No. $ Annual Income

7. OTHER INCOME OR PROPERTY

8. ANY ASSETS TRANSFERRED TO OTHERS DURING THE
   PAST FIVE YEARS

_____   Dated at Toronto this   day of   19 _
   Witness

   Witness   Signed

This form to be witnessed by two persons

_____
Social Service Interviewer

_____
Home for the Aged Interviewer

HFA 57 — 4/75

There is no requirement that homes for the aged provide extended care units, although they may if licensed to do so by the minister. In fact, however, many do provide extended care as well as "intermediate care."

Rest homes may accept any person:
(a) who is twenty-one or older and who in the opinion of two doctors, is in need of long-term maintenance and supervision, or
(b) who is under twenty-one and eligible under clause (a) whose admission is approved by the minister.

The regulations go on to clarify clause (a) by stating that any person (a) mentally or physically handicapped due to birth defects, accident, deterioration or the results of disease so that he is unable to care for himself or to be cared for in his own home; (b) who has an underlying disease process or need for complex control and his presence will not create a health hazard; (c) is not psychopathic or does not have an aggression problem; and (d) who, if admitted to a home will not be deprived of any care, benefit or protection available to him in a hospital, may be admitted to a rest home. The emphasis in rest homes is on supervision and maintenance, not on nursing and personal health care although most of the regulations applying to homes for the aged also apply to rest homes.

Since nursing homes are private operations, admission is a matter of contract between the resident and the licensee. However, provincial regulations state "where the physical or mental condition of a person is such that the person cannot properly be cared for in a nursing home, the person shall not be admitted or remain as a resident." Further, a person shall not be admitted as a resident without his consent, or where he is mentally or physically unable to give his consent, the consent of his next of kin or legal representative. A resident also may not be admitted to an extended care unit unless he qualifies for extended care payments from OHIP.

The type of person admitted is a good indication of the type of care offered in a home. It is clear from the statute and regulations that "extended" and "intermediate" care are available in a nursing home. It is also a requirement that homes give nursing care in accordance with needs. Homes may accept residents confined to bed, but since all admissions are subject to approval of the minister, care equivalent to hospital care may be difficult to find in a nursing home, given the expense of that type of care and the stringent requirements of the act and regulations.

The story of the practical nurse is told by Studs Terkel in *Working* (Avon ed.; New York: The Hearst Corp., 1975), pp. 650-655. The experience in staff-resident participation is set out by Dr. H. Grauer in "Institutions for The Aged-Therapeutic Communities?" 19, *Journal of The American Geriatrics Society*, 687 (1971); see also H. Grauer, "A Geriatric Functional Rating Scale to Determine The Need for Institutional Care," 23, *Journal of The American Geriatrics Society*, 472 (1975).

Extended Care: Limited Care

See, *Ontario Patient Care Classification* (Toronto: Ministry of Health, 1976), p. 6:

Extended Care

Definition:

Is [the kind of care] required by a person with a relatively *stabilized* (physical or mental) chronic disease or functional disability, who, having reached the apparent *limit of his recovery*, is not likely to change in the near future, who has relatively little need for the diagnostic and therapeutic services of the hospital but who requires availability of personal care on a continuing 24-hour basis, with medical and professional nursing supervision and provision for meeting psycho-social needs. The period of time during which care is required is unpredictable but usually consists of a matter of months or years.

Patient Characteristics (criteria):

1. Diagnosis has been established.
2. The patient has a chronic disease or a functional disability.
3. As demonstrated by previous assessment and response to treatment *there is little or no rehabilitation potential*.
4. The disease process is relatively stabilized.
5. There is a limited need for diagnostic and therapeutic services.
6. The individual's need is primarily availability of personal care on a continuing 24-hour basis with professional nursing supervision, limited skilled nursing techniques and medical services appropriate to the patient's needs.
7. A prolonged period of care is anticipated, i.e., the patient's condition is expected to remain significantly unchanged in the near future.

Programme Description:

This is a reactivation-oriented maintenance care program on a 24-hour basis with continuing medical and professional nursing supervision, which aims to maintain the health status and functional capacity of the individual. The program should encourage and maintain independence in activities of daily living and meet the psycho-social needs of the individual.

Activation or reactivation implies stimulation of the individual whereby physical, mental and social abilities are improved to the individual's optimum level and maintained.

To meet the psycho-social needs of the individual, there must be administrative leadership to ensure involvement of the patient, staff, family, and community.

In addition to the basic living requirements such as room and board, the program makes provision for:
1. continuous care with medical and professional nursing supervision;*
2. limited skilled nursing techniques;
3. mechanical aids for patient care, such as grab-bars, wheelchairs and walkers, etc;
4. social and recreational services;
5. part-time consultant P.T. and O.T. services available;
6. special diets;
7. drugs and medical supplies.

*Professional nursing supervision: a professional nurse is responsible for total patient care, however much of the care will actually be provided by auxiliary staff.

Costs:

The Ontario Health Insurance Plan subsidy $13.60, Personal co-payment is $7.40 (for ward), $12.10 (semi-private), $16.80 (private). This is only for extended care.

Nursing Homes are free to charge what they please for intermediate care (less than 1½ hours/day). An estimate in Ontario is $16 to $17 per day for intermediate care. Provincial regulations require that 75% of all beds be reserved for extended care. Currently 94% of the province's beds are being used for extended care (estimate by Ontario Nursing Home Association).

Issue:

A flat fee ($21) is charged for all those receiving extended care. Whether a resident requires 1½ hours of care or five hours of care a day, the nursing home in either case is going to receive the same amount of money. This creates an obvious incentive to favour admitting only those whose condition is likely to require the bare minimum of care necessary to justify imposing extended care rate. (The Ontario Nursing Home Association strongly opposes this method of reimbursement.)

Alternative:

In Manitoba there are seven different levels of care (beginning with approximately ½ hour/day of care through five levels of extended care.):
—hostel care
—personal care
—extended care 1-5.
Each level of care, of course, receives a commensurate subsidy.

Quebec has a four-tier classification system, ranging from mere lodging and social protection to care which includes a minimum of 17.5 hours of nursing attention per week, comprising 1.5 hours by a registered nurse, 2.5 by a registered nursing assistant and 13.5 hours by a nursing aide.

The United States originally had a very flexible reimbursement scheme (through its medicare and medicaid programmes) to accomodate personal care requirements. Fraudulent padding of medical bills resulted and a new federal regulation now sets out an approach similar to that in Ontario.

Even before the Bill of Rights cited in the text another was proposed in a *Report of The Ontario Council of Health: A Review of the Ontario Health Insurance Plan* (Toronto: Ontario Council of Health, 1973), p. 27:

Patient Bill of Rights — Example to Demonstrate the Concept

Inasmuch as the goal of professional medical care is the health and well-being of all the individuals requiring such care, the following "patient rights" may be formally specified:

The Right to Treatment

1) The right to appropriate medical care and equipment regardless of race, creed or income class.

The Right to Explanations

2) The right to know, or request, the significance of medical diagnoses and the nature and effect of medical treatment prescribed as a result of such diagnoses.

Rights in Medical Institutions

3) The right in medical institutions to maintain civil liberties so long as such right does not interfere with medical treatment of the patient concerned or any other patient and/or the required functions of medical staff.

The Right to Privacy

4) The right to priority treatment of any illness classifiable as an emergency and to early consultation of any condition judged as acute.

The Right to Emergency Treatment

5) The right to priority treatment of any illness classifiable as an emergency and to early consultation of any condition judged as acute.

The Right to Explanation of Bills and Fees

6) The right on request of patient to explanation of all bills and fees charged to him.

NOTES: Chapter Four

1. Loneliness: The Lost Person

The poem is by an unknown person. It was sent to Karen Moser, of the *Ottawa Journal Medical Reporter*, from a "concerned citizen." Ms. Moser used the poem to introduce a lengthy article dealing with Ottawa nursing homes. Ms. Moser wrote in part:

> A *Journal* survey of some Ottawa nursing homes revealed that not all nursing staff lacks empathy nor do all abuse their patients. . . . Unfortunately, the visits also turned up some appalling nursing home conditions, which, when brought to the attention of the Ministry of Health in Toronto received rapid investigation. . . . It was discovered that nursing homes have a weekend "dumping" system, which means they deposit sick patients on the doorsteps of local emergency wards hoping the hospital personnel will look after patients which their reduced weekend staff cannot handle. . . . It was further discovered that many such patients suffer from fecal impactions, a condition resulting from inappropriate diet coupled with inadequate exercise resulting in a complicated constipation problem that only a hospital trained staff and equipment can relieve [The Ottawa *Journal*, March 8, 1976, p. 22].

See D. Clark, "A Matter of Caring," *Canadian Welfare* (July-August 1974), p. 16 ff.:

> Other writers go on in the same vein. One middle-aged lady says, of her elderly uncle, that he has changed so greatly since entering a nursing home that it breaks her heart. He has gone completely into his shell; hardly talks when she goes to see him. He used to be a cheerful, outgoing person.
>
> From a male correspondent:
> "Real hardship starts when a person gets helpless enough to be confined in the infirmary. Quite often these people do not get all that much extra care, and this causes much suffering. I have seen this and I am sure many of the nurses would admit that the problem is urgent, and that finding the solution is urgent.
>
> "On the other hand, I would not put all the blame on the nurses. They are professionals but, having their own personal problems, are liable to get short-tempered at times and make wrong decisions."

Other letters take up the case for nurses and their aides, pointing out that nursing homes are sometimes short-staffed, which could account for some of the callousness.

One correspondent, herself a nurse, protests:
"First of all we strive daily to have compassion and give people in our care a little pleasure and some small joys to look forward to. . . . Certainly I have allowed guests to see a pet dog when requested.

"To staff a nursing home with really caring and loving attendants is a dream many hope can be attained. . . . I feel very sad about this man's letter. I fear we are a long way from being able to produce all of the joys of a true home atmosphere in our institutions.

See also H. Grauer, Institutions for the Aged: Therapeutic Communities?" 19, *Journal of The American Geriatrics Society* (1971), 687.

2. Of Prisons and "Homes": An Analogy

Reports relating to prison disturbances include: *Alberta Inquiry Into The Alleged Excessive Use of Force At The Calgary Correctional Institute*, August 23, 1973; *Report of The Commission of Inquiry Into Certain Disturbances at Kingston Prison During April, 1971* (Ottawa: Information Canada, 1973); *Report of The Solicitor General's Working Group on Federal Maximum Security Designs* (Ottawa: Information Canada, 1971).

See *Summary of First Ontario Residents' Councils Conference* (Toronto: Ministry of Community and Social Services, 1973).

The conference pointed its discussion toward recommendations. It cannot be said that government attempted in any manner to inhibit discussion. The conference was composed primarily of residents in old age facilities. Still, the fact remains that very little of the conference discussion went to the essentials of life in the institution. The conference participants did have recommendations which were passed without dissent:

Be it resolved that the words "Charitable" and "Institutions" should be eliminated from reference to the homes;

—that the term Homes for the Aged be replaced by Senior Citizens Homes;

—that the provincial government be petitioned to review its regulations regarding vacations for Residents in Homes for the Aged;

—that Residents have representation at the Annual Convention of the Homes for the Aged Conference [It was recommended this representation be made through the planning committee of the Residents' Council Conference];

—the administrator of a trust fund should let each Resident who has money in the trust fund know the balance and accumulated interest at least once every six months [All these resolutions were passed by the delegates].

3. Surrender of Choice:

The adjuvant is emphasized only as an example. It demonstrates government's intent to make specialists out of generalists, and in the process to cause the staff to become even more removed and remote from the home residents. The qualifications for becoming an adjuvant are:

Present (government) policy states that only Home employees of at least 6 months standing may be eligible for adjuvant (helper) training. The most successful trainee almost certainly has a practical nursing background, and a Grade 10 or better education.

Most important is the kind of personality the (helper) projects. Traditionally these are the warm and thoughtful staff members who display a genuine interest in residents. In addition, however, (helpers) must be able to learn new methods. They must be able to communicate well with staff as well as residents if they are to take their proper place in the Care Team. . . .

For Mr. Fletcher, a stroke victim, the adjuvant is a specialist seen for a particular purpose. Mr. Fletcher on any given day will be taken from his room by an employee, whose job calls for portering, to the adjuvant's facilities. Government has stated:

Portering of wheel-chair residents is time-consuming and can be done by any number of people in the Home. Time spent by an Adjuvant in portering is time lost from activation functions. Moreover, it is obviously useful and a necessary duty which can be delegated elsewhere, perhaps as an ego-boosting measure.

Government struggles to make adjuvants aware of their unique function. Mr. Fletcher, subject to the personal contact of a caring person — the primary characteristic of the adjuvant — might flourish. Both he and the adjuvant might develop a warm, feeling relationship. For Mr. Fletcher this is important, for he is no short-term visitor to the home. He, like nearly every other resident, once admitted to the home, will live there all of his remaining days.

But the adjuvant runs a programme and this is the warning issued by government:

> An adjuvant problem which frequently arises is that of moving the resident who has reached his potential for improvement to other programmes. The benefits are obvious. The resident needs a greater challenge, and a more needy resident can take his place in the adjuvant group. But in fact, this is often a difficult process. The resident sees himself as able to maintain his present improvement only with adjuvant help, and this intimate group has given him a very real sense of identity and worth. In addition, the adjuvant may well be, quite humanly, reluctant to lose a "star pupil". . . . Clearly each (adjuvant and resident) needs the assistance of other members of the team. Once it has been decided by all concerned that no further gain is to be obtained by his remaining in the adjuvant group, the resident should be assisted to move gradually into other activities. Department heads and personnel, aware of the change to be effected, can each in his or her own way help the adjuvant by supporting and encouraging the resident in his new venture into crafts and other activities.

See *Role of The Adjuvant in Ontario's Homes for The Aged* (Toronto: Senior Citizens' Bureau, 1974).

4. A View from The Outside

See *Report of Ontario Task Force on Long Term Care* (Toronto: Queen's Printer, 1974), pp. 71-73. A later government report used the failure to provide the programme indicated as a basis for challenging the uniform compensation provided by the province, See *Report of The Ontario Interministerial Committee on Residential Services to the Cabinet Committee on Social Development* (Toronto: Queen's Printer, 1975), pp. 49-50.

It is a curious matter for government to use its own prior-established policy as a basis for challenging another well-established policy. It is even more curious when it is recognized that the very same government, the same party in power, established both policies. The rationale, however, may be quite simple: government had the money to spend earlier. It does not now have the same wealth, and accordingly must find a justification for a change in policy.

NOTES: Chapter Five

1. A Cruel Hoax: The Quebec Experience

Mr. Novick's comments are set out in *Proceedings of the Institute on Long Term Care,* co-sponsored by the Ontario Hospital Association, Ontario Association of Homes for the Aged, Ontario Nursing Home Association, December 2-3, 1974 (Toronto: OHA Centre) pp. 82-94. Mr. Novick also emphasized the role of home care. In part he said (p. 89):

> It should be pointed out that private organizations such as the Victorian Order of Nurses, Le Société des Infirmières Visiteuses and Le Service des Soins à Domicile, which offer non-institutional home services on a short-term basis, could be induced by the community health departments to expand their programs in the future in order to include services on a long-term basis as well.
>
> Co-ordinating the work of the home-care centres, hospital centres for long-term patients, community health departments of the seven general hospitals and the local community service centres within Region 6A [Montreal], is the Council of Health and Social Services of Metropolitan Montreal, whose functions, as set forth in Chapter 48 include the following:—
> 1). to advise and assist the establishments in the preparation of their programs of development and operation of health services and social services.
> 2). to promote the setting up of common services for such establishments, the exchange of services between them, the elimination of duplication of services and a better apportionment of services in the region.
> 3). to encourage the participation of the population in defining its own needs in health services and social services and in the administration and operation of the establishment providing such services.
>
> While thus recognizing the imperative of developing a network of non-institutional long-term services within Region 6A and in the other regions of Quebec, the Department of Social Affairs nevertheless recognizes that more home-care centre beds must be provided immediately to meet the needs of people whose physical condition entitles them to receive care in an appropriate institution setting. Hundreds of such people have been waiting longer than

two years for admission into an institution. . . . At the beginning of 1974, the Department made the decision that during the course of this year, 840 additional home-care centre beds would be developed in Region 6A.

The underground homes were exposed by D. Braid in a series of three articles beginning January 19, 1976 in the *Montreal Star*. One of the essential points made by Mr. Braid is that with limited rent subsidy individuals might find their own survival. See his article on January 21, 1976. It describes a couple living in a rent-subsidized apartment for $87 a month. According to Mr. Braid, most individuals prefer such an arrangement. If adequate support services are provided (e.g. meals on wheels, domestic help, transportation to clinic), many who would otherwise require nursing home care could remain in their own homes.

There is currently a two-year waiting list for such subsidized apartments.

Only sixteen out of a planned thirty-five local community service centres exist in Montreal creating a shortage of home care services. (According to one estimate there are only twenty-five active employees working in this field, although charitable organizations also assist.)

Quebec is currently building nursing homes with a capacity of 3,500 beds (84% of which will be in Montreal). Estimate of need: beds for 6% of those over 65 (at present there are beds for 4.5%).

2. A Different Path: The Ontario Experience

Government policy encouraging larger, rather than smaller homes is gleaned from an examination of *The Toronto Star* and *The Globe and Mail* at the relevant time. The statistics speak eloquently of the government's policy. Yet, in all fairness, the specific denial of the director under the Ontario Nursing Home Act must be recorded. "He denied categorically stating that the compensation scale was designed with larger corporations in mind" [Letter from the Ontario ombudsman to Professor Baum, March 21, 1977, p. 3].

The Ontario legislation governing nursing homes does seem to imply a certain open quality. The reality is quite different. Records of hearings are not easily available. Barriers are put in the way of their examination.

The director under the Ontario Nursing Home Act did supply a listing of complaints received by his inspectors and the action they took. Unfortunately, to get the list a pledge of "*strict* confidentiality" had to be given. What an odd situation! The director provided *twenty-two pages* of itemized complaints that said next to nothing. They listed the date of the complaint; the nature of the complaint; result of investigation; and action taken.

The director seemed so anxious to protect his information that the categories were generalized to absurdity. For example, without, we feel, violating our pledge, there is the following entry: "Nature of complaint — Fast Staff Turnover; Result of Investigation — Partially Justified; Action Taken — Situation rectified prior to investigation."

We are told nothing about the nature of the staff turnover. Nor are we told about the effect of the turnover on residents. Nor are we told the reasons for the turnover. Nor are we told what action the administration took to correct the problem.

The real nature of compliance with statute and regulations might well have been exposed by the Ottawa *Journal*. In March 1976 the paper focused upon MacLaren House, a nursing home for 100 in Ottawa. The *Journal* noted the dismal environment in which the residents lived. It noted the difficulty the Ministry of Health experienced in obtaining compliance with its own inspection reports and orders. Three months later there appeared the following article. See D. Rogers, "Nursing Home Gets Ultimatum," the Ottawa *Citizen*, May 21, 1976:

> The MacLaren House nursing home at 207 MacLaren St. could face a $2,000 fine or loss of its licence by June 15 if it does not make improvements requested by the Ontario Ministry of Health. A spokesman for the government won't close the home but has sent in inspectors following complaints. The home said Friday it is impossible to make the home look new because it was converted from an apartment building nine years ago and was not intended as a nursing home. Ms. Blostein admitted the ministry wants improvements in patient supervision, recreation, personal grooming and record keeping. . . . "This place is pretty drab," said Ms. Blostein. "We know — we are not blind. It is physically impossible to improve this nursing home without bringing in a lot of workers."
>
> The 100 patients at the home must do without many things most of them had in their own homes. There are some plastic flowers but few real plants because Ms. Blostein says many are poisonous and could harm senile patients who might eat them. . . . Patients in wheelchairs can't leave their rooms without assistance because of high marble door knobs. Most sleep two or three to a room and don't get out much, especially during the winter. . . . Many rooms have small adjoining kitchens but the stoves are disconnected where it is feared patients might injure themselves. . . . Furniture is sparse and there are few television sets. One staff member said the elderly patients don't enjoy television. . . . There are several sunrooms but the patients cannot use the home's backyard because the only door to it leads from the kitchen which is out of bounds to them. . . . Air conditioning is not used, said

Ms. Blostein, because old people don't get hot. She said many residents ask for extra blankets during hot summer weather.

George Newell, the Canadian Union of Public Employees representative for most of the 85 nursing home workers, said he is deeply concerned about the pressure being put on the home to make improvements.

"The Ministry of Health is raising hell about this place but doesn't do it elsewhere," said Mr. Newell. "This seems like an excessive amount of pressure."

After necessary changes had been made the home was placed on the market for sale for about $1.5 million. See K. Moser, "MacLaren House-Nursing Home Up for Sale," the Ottawa *Journal*, July 9, 1976.

The key to the proper operation of any home is its *staff* and the *quality of life* provided. What follows is a summary of some provincial regulations dealing with both, and the Ontario use of legislative sanctions to compel enforcement:

KEY STAFF REQUIREMENTS
Homes for the Aged and Rest Homes

Every home in Ontario is to be headed by an administrator appointed by City Council, or appointed by a management board of the home, which itself is appointed by the lieutenant-governor in council. By s.11(1) the administrator has to have completed a course of instruction approved by the minister. The Revised Regulations of Ontario 1970, Reg. 439, s. 2 states that an administrator must: "a) be in good health, b) have a specialized knowledge of and adequate experience in modern methods of administering a home, c) have a sympathetic understanding of problems pertaining to the needs of elderly persons residing in a home and a suitable personality for the position, and d) have the ability to retain the confidence of the staff and to direct it efficiently." The functions of an administrator are many and include the buying of food for residents, filing reports with the minister, keeping trust accounts for those residents who request it, and more duties which in fact give him near complete administrative control over the home.

The staff of a home comprises "such staff as the administrator shall require" (s.11[3]), but a home for the aged must have "a nurse registered under the Nurses Act" (RRO, Reg. 439, s.3). Rest homes must be supervised twenty-four hours a day by a nurse registered under the Nurses Act with one nurse per forty residents between 8:00 A.M. and midnight, and one nurse per sixty residents from midnight until 8:00 A.M. (Ont. Reg. 439, RRO 1970, s. 41). By section 11(4) of the Act, the municipal council (or board of management) shall, with the approval of the minister, appoint a licensed doctor as the physician for the home "who is responsible for the medical care and services provided to the residents." A resident of the home may avail himself of a private doctor (presumably at his own expense), but by s. 18(2) of Reg. 439, "all medical and paramedical services, programs, procedures and medications provided or used in a home are subject to the approval of the physician of the home." Absent from the statute and regulations is any provision to the effect that only the licensed nurse or doctor may administer medication, although only the doctor for the home or the private attending doctor may prescribe medication.

Nursing Homes

Every nursing home in Ontario must have an administrator who by s.75 of Ont. Reg. 196/72 "is responsible for its administration and who shall be deemed an employee" of the home. That regulation also provides that the administrator must be at least eighteen, free of any communicable disease, willing to undergo mental and physical tests as to his fitness to work in a home, a high school diploma or "satisfactory" work experience. The requirements of the licensee were discussed above. An administrator shall not administer more than two homes at one time.

The licensee by s.45 of Ont. Reg. 196/76 shall obtain an advisory physician who shall advise the administrator as to the medical and nursing services of the home. The resident or his legal representative or, if he can't afford one, the administrator shall retain a physician to attend the resident and provide him with medical care by s.46(1). By s.48, "the administrator shall make arrangements for a physician to be on call to provide emergency services when a resident's physician or substitute physician is not available."

A nursing home must have a nursing staff. Section 51 requires each resident to be given nursing care in accordance with his needs and the care being given under supervision of a registered nurse who is Director of Nurses (s.55), and there shall be a registered nurse on call at all times. In the extended care units, a registered nurse shall be on *duty* during each shift. Section 57 requires only one nurse or nursing assistant per twelve to twenty residents (depending on the time of day) in an extended care unit where the residents need only one and one half hours of nursing and personal care each day. (This should be compared with Alberta Reg. 197/71, s.21[2] promulgated under the Nursing Home Act RSA 1970, c.264. Here there need be only one nurse for every seventy-five patients.)

QUALITY OF LIFE

Homes for the Aged and Rest Homes

Section 15 of the Act provides: "The council of a municipality having a home . . . shall provide such equipment and materials as will enable the residents of the home or joint home to engage in handicrafts and other such occupations."

> Section 5 of RRO 439 provides that the administrator shall:
> (m) ensure that an adequate supply of books, other published material and current periodicals and newspapers is available to residents at all times.
> (n) ensure that there are adequate and regular opportunities in the home for residents who so desire to participate in religious services. . . .
> (p) establish and follow a regular procedure for the hearing of any grievance of any resident of the home, correct the grievance if he considers it necessary and maintain a written record of all such hearings. . . .
> (s) co-operate in any program established under The Elderly Persons Centres Act which could be of benefit or interest to the residents of the home.

Section 8(1) (RRO 439) provides that no resident shall leave the home without notifying the administrator or his representative. Presumably, under s.7(RRO 439) the administrator could refuse to let the resident leave. Under s.8(3) a resident may sell any article he makes while in the home and keep the proceeds. A resident cannot smoke except in designated areas and cannot have liquor without the consent of the administrator. A resident may leave money in trust with the administrator but the administrator must keep strict written account of any such money and return it to the resident when requested (s.33 of RRO 439). An administrator must be bonded by s.36(RRO 439). There are no provisions for the use of restraining devices, but there can be a medical "service" which could be approved for use by a physician under s.18(1) (RRO 439). A resident may be discharged pursuant to s. 17 of the Act when, in the opinion of the physician for the home, the resident is no longer eligible to stay, or it is in his interest to be discharged.

Nursing Homes

By section 13(1) of O Reg. 196/72 every nursing home has to have a sitting room. Each home also shall "(1) in addition to the sitting room or rooms provide adequate and suitable areas for crafts and activity programs. (2) all equipment for such areas shall be suitable for such activities in a nursing home. (3) activity areas shall have a minimum floor area calculated at the rate of six feet per bed in the home.''

Section 68 of Ontario Reg. 196/72 provides: ''the licensee of a nursing home shall designate members of the nursing home staff who shall establish and implement on a regular basis organized programs of social, physical and recreational activities suitable for the residents who are able to participate in such programs.'' Also it provides that nurses shall keep extensive written records of who participated in these programs, the date and time of participation, etc. Subsection (3) of this section requires each nursing home to keep available, without charge to the resident, books, current magazines and newspapers, games, supplies and equipment for crafts, radio and television.

The administrator of a nursing home must keep extensive records of any money given in trust by the resident. The resident is not required to deposit any money with the administrator, and the administrator must return any money given in trust on demand of the resident or any trustee acting on behalf of the resident (O Reg. 196/72, s.93).

A restraining apparatus may be applied to a resident on a physician's approval after having attended to him (O Reg. 196/72, s.50[1]). The apparatus must be examined at least once an hour by a registered nurse or registered nursing assistant (O Reg. 508/72, s.13).

There are no restrictions on the comings and goings of residents or their guests, nor any requirements as to sleep (minimums or maximums).

Provisions from other provinces are worth noting here. The Saskatchewan provision reads as follows (Sask. Reg. 34/66):

3(d) No operator, member of the management, nor person employed by the operator or management of a home shall accept, without permission from the director, a power of attorney from a guest in the said home.
6(b) Guests shall at all times show evidence of adequate care:
(i) Criteria for determining adequate care shall include appearance of good personal hygiene such as clean, healthy appearing skin, clean trimmed fingernails and toe nails, clean and neatly groomed hair, clean teeth and mouth, and an absence of cracked lips.
(vii) evidence of an attempt to create as cheerful and home-like an environment as possible;
(viii) evidence of kind and considerate care;
(ix) evidence that guests are encouraged to be up and dressed in their own personal clothing for at least a brief period every day, unless ordered otherwise by a doctor.
(c) The operator shall, whenever possible, segregate guests in a

home to accommodate them with guests who have similar interests and are in a comparable state of health and aging.

10(a) The home shall arrange for or provide individual and group activities, recreational and diversional opportunities suited to the needs and interests of its guests. Participation in any such activity shall be voluntary.

(b) Guests shall have free access to recreational areas and shall not be required to remain in their rooms unless so ordered by their physician. *Some activities and recreational opportunities shall be made available to guests who are unable to leave their rooms.*

(d) Guests shall be permitted to leave the home to visit, shop, or engage in other social activities unless good cause can be shown for refusing such permission.

Alberta Reg. 197/71 s.23(2) provides: "Each contract nursing home shall arrange for or provide individual and group activities, recreational and diversional opportunities suited to the needs and interests of its patients" (see Sask. Reg. 34/66 s.10[a]).

3. Inspection: A Study of Limitations

Legislative Sanctions

There are only three legislative sanctions available:
1. Fine for violating the Act or regulations.
2. Examination of employees' physical and mental fitness to work in a home.
3. Revocation of licence.

Should receivership be a part of an Act? It already is under Ontario law applicable to nursing homes in sections 11 and 12. If the home's licence is revoked or expires and the minister refuses to renew it, the licensee is entitled to a hearing. Pending the outcome of that hearing the minister may occupy and operate the home on the order of a High Court judge (s.11).

If, after the hearing and any appeal, the licence remains revoked, the minister may occupy and operate the home for the purpose of arranging alternative accomodation for those in the home (s.12[2]). The occupation may last for only six months.

A receivership procedure is then clearly contemplated by the Act. The question then becomes should the procedure be expanded? Should the receivership become a permanent thing? It would be in effect an expropriation for which, according to the Expropriation Act of Ontario, just compensation would have to be paid. (There is in Canada no constitution or provision to pay compensation.) However, couldn't the payment be made incrementally out of the profits of the home, for the homes are clearly profitable? . . . In this way the residents would not suffer the trauma of relocation and the licensee's offending practices could be ended.

Perhaps a provision could be grafted onto the Act requiring the government (during the receivership it can have at present) to procure a buyer for the home at a fair price. The buyer might be allowed to pay for the home out of its profits. This way the residents would not suffer, the former licensee would get his money and the home would stay in private hands.

The Act and the regulations provide little in the way of standards of behaviour for the administrator and the employees. Ontario Reg. 1976/72, ss. 75-81 merely lay out basic qualifications for administrators and employees. The fine and the examinations by the director are all that threaten the security of the administrator (who is an employee) and the other employees. Shouldn't they be charged with carrying out the requirements of the Act under the same standard of care with which a trustee is required to perform his duties? In view of the extremely delicate emotional condition of many residents, infraction of the requirements (even though not sufficient grounds for a fine or examination) should be grounds for disciplinary action.

Statistics: Ontario Institutions
for the Elderly

NURSING HOMES

1966	501 homes	11,500 beds
1972	481 homes	22,200 beds
		(75% *v* extended care)
1974	416 homes	23,500 beds
		(88% *v* extended care)
1975	385 homes	25,452 beds
		(94% *v* extended care)

1,700 new beds approved for 1976 licensing based on number over 65 in given area.
Turnover of residents — complete turnover every four years.

Summary for Homes for the Aged

HOMES FOR THE ELDERLY

(as of May 31, 1976)

	; of homes	total beds	res. care	extended care	% extended care to total
Municipal Homes	88	17,861	8,027	9,834	55.1
Charitable Homes	86	9,059	6,605	2,454	27.1

Provincial Averages: *:* OF Beds/Home
    Municipal Homes   203
    Charitable Homes   105

	TOTAL MALES	TOTAL FEMALES
Municipal Homes	5,820	10,698
Charitable Homes	2,012	5,770

EXTENDED CARE

	Males in Extended Care	% Males in Extended Care	Females in Extended Care	% Females in Extended Care
Municipal Homes	2,668		5,793	
Charitable Homes	524		1,609	

RESIDENTIAL CARE

	Males	% Males	Females	% Females
Municipal Homes	3,152	39.6	4,805	60.4
Charitable Homes	1,488	26.8	4,161	73.2

DEATHS

(during 1974)

	TOTAL	MALE	FEMALE
Municipal Homes	2,126	824	1,302
Charitable Homes	517	134	383

NOTES: Chapter Six

1. Streaming The Aged: From Hospitals to "Homes"

The relevant extended care data was drawn from the lengthy appendix in *A Report of the Ontario Health Insurance Plan* (Toronto: Ontario Council of Health 1973) p. 59.

It is useful to ask why government is so stringent in compensating for paramedical services. The amounts are not likely to be that great. Physicians' offices are already overcrowded. Indeed, there are areas where there are *no* physicians. Yet, curiously, part of the answer can be found in the desire of the medical profession to keep a monopoly of its industry. See generally, I. Illich, *Limits to Medicine-Medical Nemesis: The Expropriation of Health* (Toronto: McClelland & Stewart, 1976), pp. 41-43. More specifically, the Health Committee stated in the *Annual Report of the Ontario Advisory Council on Senior Citizens* (1975-1976), p. 21:

> The Health Committee met with officials from the Ministry of Health regarding foot care. This area is of great concern to the Committee as a whole and individual members felt very strongly that something should be done to alleviate the situation. The following areas were of special concern:
>
> —the billing practices of podiatrists particularly where extra billing to the patient is permitted in addition to OHIP payments;
>
> —the need for procedural guidelines for podiatrists in order to control the dispensing of medications, the over-use of x-rays and the need for surgical intervention as a method of treatment;
>
> —the monopolistic attitude on the part of some podiatrists toward the market;
>
> —the great need for foot care professionals (whatever they may be called);
>
> There are 80 practising podiatrists in the province at the present time. The estimated need is 450.
>
> In the light of the foregoing, the following recommendation was made:
>
> WHEREAS there are planned revisions in the Health Disciplines regarding Chiropody; and

WHEREAS there is presently a great scarcity of trained foot care specialists; and

WHEREAS registered nursing personnel are presently giving excellent foot care to many elderly people

Therefore the Ontario Advisory Council on Senior Citizens recommends that:

For the interim and until such time as qualified foot care specialists can be prepared in the province, (earliest date 1979) Registered Nurses and Registered Nursing Assistants be instructed in a specific "upgrading" course in foot care and that this service be made easily available (accessible) to seniors in Elderly Persons Centres, Day Centres, clinics, community health centres.

The data relating to chronic hospital beds is somewhat confusing. One government document speaks of a total of 10.5 per cent of the population as being over 65 and an 8 per cent *increase* in chronic hospital beds. (Report of the *Ontario Task Force on Long Term Care* [Toronto: Queen's Printer, 1974], p. 133.) Another, more recent report sets forth the information contained in the text. See *Report of the Ontario Interministerial Committee on Residential Services to the Cabinet Committee on Social Development* (Toronto: Queen's Printer, 1975), p. 68.

Government has the means to alter radically the extended care programme. By administrative regulation, rather than statute, government may modify its extended care programme in important ways.

It is provided in *The Health Insurance Act*, Statutes of Ontario 1972, s. 51(i) that "The Lieutenant Governor in Council may make regulations, . . . (i) prescribing the services rendered in or by hospitals and health facilities and by practitioners that are insured services: A health facility is specifically defined in S. 1(f) of the Act as including extended care units in a nursing home. . . ."

Ontario Regulation 323/72 defines extended care services in S. 41(1). Among the services included in the definition is "skilled nursing care" which is defined in Ontario Regulation 196/72 (under *the Nursing Homes Act*) as a minimum of 1½ hours of nursing care. In S. 41(3) of Ontario Regulation 323/72 it is provided that the government shall pay $9 per resident per day to each nursing home for extended care services provided. (This figure has increased since 1972).

It is clear, therefore, that the regulations promulgated under the *Health Insurance Act* prescribing the services for which OHIP will pay and how much they will be paid affect substantially the operation of a nursing home. If subsequent regulations were drafted under the Health Insurance Act redefining extended services more narrowly and cutting back the amount the government would pay for those services, the nursing homes in Ontario would directly be affected.

2. Re-Evaluation: Cutting Back

The method of financing extended care provides perhaps a way to understand the level of benefits. "A Review of the Ontario Health Insurance Plan," *The Report of the Ontario Council of Health* (Senior Advisory Body to the Minister of Health), (Toronto: Ontario Council of Health 1973), pp. 68-69 sets out the comparisons summarized in chart form on pages 164 to 169.

3. Squeezing The Old: New Charges

The data for this section, and for much of the chapter, is derived from the *Report of The Ontario Interministerial Committee on Residential Services to the Cabinet Committee on Social Development* (Toronto: Queen's Printer, 1975). In many respects it is a fallacy to call this document a "report." It consists of several study memoranda, prepared in 1975, and kept secret for about two years. Then with a certain fanfare the document was released to the public with a view toward encouraging discussion. However, only a limited number of documents, detailed, complex, and often confusing were prepared for distribution, and their sale price at $18 each has not encouraged public purchase.

The inconsistencies in public policy were too much even for the bureaucratic mind. The report stated (p. 36)

> These variations (in charges and programmes) appear to result in situations which are not only in conflict, but are also inexplicable to the general public" [Italics in the text].

For example, comparisons can be made between situations in which
—the charges for government services decrease as the amount of service increases;

—The poorest clients may appear to pay the highest charges.

In a letter from Bill Clapperton, Manager of Research and Planning, Ontario Nursing Home Association, to Professor Baum dated October 25, 1976, Mr. Clapperton wrote: "It may also be of interest to you that 60-65% of the total expenses incurred will be paid out in salaries. Other expenses will be food (approximately $1.50-$1.80 per resident day — this is bulk raw food cost) laundry and housekeeping items, utilities and fixed items which vary due to geographic location."

Under the authority of the Osgoode Hall Law School Public Interest Group an effort was made to obtain profit figures concerning nursing home operations from the Ministry of Health. The request was made by letter dated October 27, 1976. The ombudsman replied by letter dated March 21, 1977. While his five-page letter does not provide profit data, it does indicate that such data are available. "The memorandum [of reply to the ombudsman from the Ministry of Health] also pointed out that the Ministry does not formally request information on profitability, however, all data on costs and revenue are captured and, as a result, the industry is carefully monitored financially" [p. 4].

4. Passing The Buck: Letting Ottawa Pay

Existing security programmes are examined in some detail in D. Baum, *The Final Plateau: The Betrayal of Our Older Citizens* (Toronto: Burns & MacEachern Ltd., 1974). See especially, pp. 159-192, 228-34. The reality seems to be that Canada, as a nation, is moving toward a single pension scheme which will be funded by government. The role of the private pension seems to be diminishing. Yet the demise of the private pension cannot be taken for granted.

Keith Harvey Cooper is the President of the Canadian Pension Conference, which was formed in 1960 and has 900 members throughout Canada, a large number of whom represent industrial and financial companies with pension schemes. Mr. Cooper argues strongly that there is a role for private pensions. He believes that upward to 60 per cent of the Canadian work force — if properly counted — participate in private pension benefits. In 1977 he noted that six different studies were pending involving pensions. These studies included both government task forces and royal commissions.

> The move to a two-tiered government controlled pension system could choke off the necessary funds that our capital-hungry economy requires to sustain itself. . . . If private plans are allowed to die, where will these capital funds come from? . . . Private plans currently contribute more than $3 billion annually to the Canadian economy. . . . Public service plans actually provide greater take-home pay after retirement, particularly in the lower earning levels. . . .
>
> A civil servant retiring at age 55 after 30 years' service receives a fully indexed pension and may then get another job. . . . We can't afford this kind of nonsense [L. Welsh, *"Private Pensions Called Necessary as Source of Funds for Economy,"* The Globe and Mail, June 9, 1977, p. B-1; see, also, p. B-5].

5. This is the amount institutionalized old people are permitted to have for themselves each month. For extended care residents it is calculated as follows: OAS/GIS/GAINS plus Ontario tax credits less the co-insurance per diem.

Summary Comparison of Provincial Health Services Insurance Plans Under the Medical Care Act (Canada)

Particulars	Ontario	Br. Columbia	Alberta	Manitoba
Extended Health Care Benefits				
Method of Financing	Premiums federal and provincial contribution of appropriated funds.	Premiums federal and provincial contributions	Premiums federal and provincial contributions	General Revenue and Federal contributions
Premium Rates	Combined Monthly health insurance premiums (hospital and medical services) $11. single $22. Family	Monthly $5. Single $10. couple $12.50 Family of 3z	Combined Monthly medical and hospital $5.75 single $11.50 fam.	Combined Monthly medical and hospital $4.15 single $8.30 fam. Discontinued July 1, 1973
Est. Federal Contribution as a % of Total Shareable Cost (1972-73)	40-45%	45-50%	50-55%	50-55%

Premium Assistance	Yes	Yes	Yes	No
Full Assistance	Yes	No	No	No
	Eligible residents without taxable income in previous year receive free coverage upon application. All social assistance recipients and their eligible dependants	Except for eligible social assistance groups	Except for residents receiving assistance benefits from Department of Social Develop't. Residents aged 65 or over excused from premium payments	Except for Public Welfare recipients who are excused from premium payment and Old Age Security Pensioners who receive the maximum guaranteed income

Summary Comparison of Provincial Health Insurance Plans Under the Medical Care Act (Canada)

Saskatchewan	Quebec	New Brunswick	Nova Scotia	P.E.I.	Nfld.
Extended Health Care Benefits (Cont'd.)					
Joint tax levy for hospital & medical services. Federal and provincial contribution. JOINT TAX RATES for combined medical & hospital services. Single $36.-Family $72. per annum payable in semi-annual instalments for singles and quarterly for families. Residents of Swift Current Health Region pay only	Tax levy of 0.8% of net income up to maximum of $125. for employees if wages constitute 75% or more of net income & up to $200. for other individuals. Pay-roll tax of 0.8% of gross income levied on employers without ceiling		General Revenue and Fed. Contribution		

hospital tax
part ($24. &
$48. resp.)
To be abol-
ished effective
Jan. 1, 1974

No Prem.
60-65%

No

No

Except for
designated
social assist-
ance groups
or indigents
who are ex-
empted from
tax levy.
Same applies
to Indians
for whom the
tax levy is
paid by
government

No Prem.
50-55%

Yes

Yes

Individuals
who for the
purpose of
provincial
income tax
have the
status of
married per-
sons or the
equivalent
thereof do
not pay any
contribution

No Prem.
75-80%

No Prem.
60-65%

No Prem.
70-75%

NOT APPLICABLE
NOT APPLICABLE

No Prem.
90-95%

NOTES: Chapter Seven

1. Protection After Death

The inquest involving Mrs. Richardson was well reported in Toronto newspapers. See for example, N. Van Rijn, "Care Inadequate at Nursing Home Inquest Jury Says," *The Toronto Star*, March 5, 1977, p. A-2. Without that reporting it is highly unlikely that the community would have been aware of the problems raised before the Coroner's Court. Dr. Milton, the presiding coroner, said in her summation to the jury: "I think the newspapers have done excellent service, particularly certain ones, in trying to bring these matters to the public" [*Transcript Summation of Dr. Milton In The Coroner's Court, Municipality of Metropolitan Toronto, Inquest Into Death Of Bertha Richardson*, March 4, 1977]. It is worth noting that, but for the press reports of this important hearing, the record would not have been preserved. The record is not that transcribed and made available for study. Copies of the summation had to be ordered specially and privately purchased.

Little has been written of the coroner's function. Dr. Shulman, however, certainly provided some measure of publicity concerning that office in his book *Coroner* (Markham: Simon & Schuster Ltd., 1975). More academic statements concerning that office can be found in R.C. Bennett, "The Role of The Coroner's Office," *The Role of The Inquest in Today's Litigation* (Toronto: Law Society of Upper Canada, 1975), p. 3. Other articles in the same publication bearing upon the subject discussed in the text include: G.H.R. Cooper, "Investigation" (p. 9), and B. Affleck, "The Role of The Crown at The Inquest" (p. 21). See also E.S. Ellis, "When An Autopsy Should Be Ordered," *Basic Educational Courses for Coroners* (Toronto: Office of The Coroner, 1973). It is from the academic materials that the statistics cited have been drawn.

> (1) Where a resident dies in a nursing home his death shall be reported immediately to a coroner by the person in charge of the nursing home at the time of the resident's death and the resident's physician shall be called.
> (2) The body of the deceased resident may be moved to a suitable area in the nursing home when the attending physician is satisfied that the death was from natural causes and the coroner has been informed.
> (3) The attending physician shall make a written report indicating the cause and time of death of the resident and the report shall be retained in the deceased's file.

The following legal framework is provided by Ontario Regulation 196/72 on the death of a resident:

(4) A report of the time, date and circumstances of the death of a resident, the name and address of the person, if any, who claims the body and the date that notice of death is given to the coroner shall be attached to the deceased resident's records [Section 74(1)].

2. The coroner's budget, like that of every other agency of government, has its limitations. In the past the coroner routinely ordered autopsies into motor vehicle deaths. By 1974 he had to be more "selective" in asking for autopsies or inquests.

The Executive Officer in the Chief Coroner's Office of Ontario cautioned trainee coroners:

Cost should not be the most vital consideration in your determination as to whether an autopsy should be ordered or otherwise. Nevertheless, it has to be a factor. The monies that pay for such examinations come from tax appropriations that are paid by people like you and your neighbour. Make sure that the dollar return is worthwhile.

3. What follows are two successful fights — as seen by Dr. Shulman:

From 1952 to 1962 there were from 6 to 10 construction "trench deaths" in Toronto each year (people buried alive by landslides as a result of poor excavation shoring). In 1963, when Dr. Shulman became Chief Coroner, he instructed his staff that all construction deaths were to have an inquest, preceded by a thorough investigation. The coroner's staff acted.

Coroner's juries returned strong recommendations, such as requiring contractors to hire full-time inspectors; posting safety bonds; and laying criminal charges when there was a breach of government regulations. By the end of the summer the media highlighted the jury recommendations. Under mounting public pressure the Ministry of Labour instructed its inspectors to crack down on all construction sites and ensure compliance with regulations, particularly with respect to shoring. The situation improved and the deaths ceased simply because "the contractors had now found that it had become cheaper to shore excavations than to suffer the penalties of government fines, bad publicity, stop-work orders and criminal charges."

Until 1964 between 3 to 12 children died in Toronto each year following tonsillectomies. Every hospital had its own method of caring for the post-operative patients. Every hospital but one had had the occasional fatality. The Hospital for Sick Children had not suffered a tonsil death for over 10 years. This was attributed to a strict hospital routine. The coroner's jury brought in a series of recommendations based on the procedure used in the Hospital for Sick Children. Two days after the inquest was concluded, St. Michael's Hospital of Toronto announced it would immediately adopt all the recommendations made by the jury and within two weeks every other Toronto hospital followed suit. "Since that date to my knowledge no children have died in Toronto following tonsillectomy."

4. Caring for One Person: Doctors on Review

The investigation by the Ralph Nader study is found in C. Townsend, *Old Age: The Last Segregation* (Bantam ed. 1971, New York: Grossman Publishers). The study represents the work during 1970 of six seniors and a young instructor from Miss Porter's School in Farmington, Connecticut. It is more than a study and critique of nursing homes; it is an attempt to afford a "consumer" guide to those who would buy the services of a nursing home.

The following passage is particularly relevant to this chapter:

> For those in nursing homes, little is being done to insure that the elderly receive adequate care even when they can pay for it. The Federal government has so far failed to enforce standards for nursing homes despite overwhelming evidence that many of them are not providing proper care. Results of ineffective standard setting are not always obvious to the casual visitor who may be impressed by the thick carpets in the parlor and the color television set. Rarely does the public take a searching look at the bedrooms, bathrooms, kitchens, and therapy rooms (if any) which are the boundaries of existence for most nursing home patients."

The experience of the United States has relevance to Canada for two reasons:
(1) The legislative scheme of the United States is similar to that of the provinces.
(2) The same difficulties in shaping and enforcing decent standards exist in the United States as in Canada. What follows is a summary, not a detailed analysis.

General Facts and Statistics (United States)

(1) There are about 20,000 nursing homes of which 80 to 95% are estimated as privately operated.
(2) A federal scheme, Medicaid, pays approximately 60% of the country's $7.5 billion nursing home bills. There is no limitation as to length of stay. Medicare, also a federal programme, pays another 7% (with a limit of 100 days during any "spell of illness" or for post-hospital care services). Two-thirds of nursing home costs are thus federally subsidized.

(3) Medicaid was intended to provide medical care for the indigent. Acceptance of Medicaid reimbursements by a home forecloses it from seeking supplemental payment from the resident or his relatives. (This regulation was upheld by the Court of Appeals in *Johnson's Professional Nursing Home v. Weinberger*, 490 Federal Reporter Second Series 841 [5th Cir. 1974]).

(4) More than one million persons live in nursing homes (1971). This figure is expected to double by the end of the century. It is estimated that one elderly person (over 65) in five will spend some time in a nursing home. Approximately 5% of the country's elderly are in institutions. The average age of nursing home residents is 82, and less than half are ambulatory.

(5) A U.S. comptroller general's study in 1970 showed patient reimbursement rates varied from $4.53 to $68.17 per day, as compared to $21 in Ontario.

(6) Federal reimbursements to the States have been according to state-created formulae — either a flat daily rate per patient, as in Ontario, or a cost-plus system. Both methods were seriously abused, the former through cutting services to patients, and the latter through padding bills sent to Medicaid. (The cost-plus system was adopted by New York. See Hess, "A Growing Scandal," *New York Times*, October 7, 1974, p.1).

(7) Nursing Home care in the U.S. is administered by three types of facilities:

(a) Skilled Nursing Facilities (SNF) offer 24-hour nursing care under the supervision of a registered nurse. They are regulated by the Federal Department of Health, Education and Welfare (H.E.W.) and by the states. There are 9,000 SNFs with nearly 65,000 beds.

(b) Intermediate Care Facilities (ICF) provide health-related care to a lesser degree than SNFs. There are 4,500 such institutions with about 220,000 beds, all of which are subject to state and federal regulation. They may qualify only for Medicaid reimbursements (whereas SNF residents may also qualify under Medicare).

(c) Custodial Care Facilities provide no nursing services but rather personal care (e.g. assistance in bathing, dressing and eating). There are approximately 9,000 of these facilities, with about 250,000 beds. They are regulated exclusively by the states and are not eligible for Medicare or Medicaid reimbursements.

Serious abuses began to surface in the late 1960s (after the enactment of Medicare and Medicaid in 1965). At this time chains of franchises developed (e.g., Medicenters of America with over 60 facilities under the same management as Holiday Inns). Profits were enormous for many, though the bankruptcy in 1970 of one of the largest chains, Four Seasons Nursing Centers of America, Inc., chilled much of the early enthusiasm. Stockholder losses were estimated at $200 million.

During this period some of the high profits were, in part, attributable to the following types of abuses:

(1) There were kickbacks from funeral homes and pharmacies that received nursing home business. It was estimated that Medicaid alone spends about $200 million. One prominent author wrote: "Half of that bill is padding: That is if only the needed drugs were ordered, and if the price was right, the government would be paying out less than half what it pays now — and patients who are now drugged would be healthier." (Drugs are one of the ancillary services provided by federal and state agencies.) Often there can be interlocking ownership of homes and suppliers of ancillary services. Other ancillary services include dentists, optometrists, podiatrists, and ambulances.

(2) There were "team" visits by physicians whose services were also ancillary. They presented a $100-million annual bill to Medicaid alone for nursing home patients. Some of the same physicians had invested heavily in nursing home corporations.

(3) What skilled patient care there is, often comes from paramedics. "In the end 80% to 90% of the care is given by untrained aides and orderlies." Indeed, a Chicago study revealed that investigators hired as unskilled janitors and aides were, "within hours of beginning work, . . . administering drugs, and one was even serving as an administrator of a home" [from a U.S. Senate Subcommittee Introductory Report].

(4) Other problems relating to patient care have included: requests for assistance ignored; inadequate bathing care; failure to turn bedridden patients; bedpans not provided; and bland, cold or unwholesome food. Patients later admitted to hospitals are often dehydrated or comatose.

Regulations:

The individual states are responsible for overseeing their own nursing homes. To receive Medicaid funds, homes were required to meet both state and federal standards, but inspections to determine compliance were carried out by state officials, though the Federal Department of Health, Education and Welfare must approve the state's plan for supervising the care in its homes. Fire regulations (The Life Safety Code) are federally promulgated by the National Fire Protection Association.

This system has proved inadequate. Congressman David Pryor called it a "national farce." The estimates of how many homes were below regulatory standards range from "over 50%" (the Senate Subcommittee) to 80% (Ralph Nader). A report by the Federal General Accounting Office, published in 1971, based on the inspection of 90 homes in New York, Oklahoma and Michigan, revealed that at least 50% had serious deficiencies (e.g., 48 of the 90 surveyed lacked adequate nursing staff; 47 failed to provide adequate physician attendance; and 44 did not comply with firm safety standards).

Reforms:

(1) The most fundamental reform proposed — and one which appears in virtually every study made on the subject — is that nursing homes cease to be profit-making operations. A United States Senate subcommittee report contained this comment by a physician:

> After 15 years of research and practice, I come now to believe that the profit motive must be eliminated from our care systems. . . . The conflict between profit and service is too great to overcome. Only in the United States and Canada (to my knowledge) is there 'commercialization' . . . [Dr. Robert Butler].

The chairman of a New York legislative committee investigating nursing homes likewise concluded that a non-profit system would be preferrable to that now in existence.

Furthermore, non-commercial homes need not necessarily be administered federally (Great Britain, for example, under the National Assistance Act of 1948 *requires* local authorities to provide *and manage* the following facilities and services: chiropody service, podiatry, meals-on-wheels, home help service, occupational therapy, recuperative holidays, residential homes for mental health, home nursing, health visiting, ambulance service, day centres and clubs and residential accomodation).

Given that private homes still do exist, however, Morris Abram, chairman of the New York State Commission investigating nursing homes, proposed that independent accountants certify the books of all nursing homes "at the risk of their professional lives." More effective "medical review" has also been recommended to improve the quality of care provided by nursing homes. Medical review teams could consist of educators, nurses, therapists, social workers, and physicians. They could assess the psychological and social needs of the patient, as well as the medical needs, and devise programmes of care accordingly.

Sources:

Articles

"Long Term Care for the Elderly: the Challenge of the Next Decade," 39, *Albany Law Review*, 617 (1975); "Quality Assurance Systems in Nursing Homes," 535, *Journal of Urban Law*, 153, (1975); "An Appraisal of the Nursing Home Enforcement Process," 17, *Arizona Law Review*, 304 (1975); "The Nursing Home Morass: Likelihood of Extrication and Reform", 17, Arizona Law Review, 357 (1975).

Congressional Reports

Subcommittee on Long-Term Care of the Senate Special Committee on Aging, *Nursing Home Care in the U.S.: Failure in Public Policy, Introductory Report*, S. Rep. No. 93-1420, 93rd Cong., 2d Sess. 1-2 (1974). (This report is the first of a proposed 12 volumes by the subcommittee probing long-term nursing care.)

Subcommittee on Long-Term Care of the Senate Special Committee on Aging, 93rd Cong., 2d Sess., *Nursing Home Care in the U.S.: Failure in Public Policy, Supporting Paper No. 1, The Litany of Nursing Home Abuses and an Examination of the Roots of Controversy* (Comm. Print 1974). This volume cites specific abuses to patients, poor physical conditions and frauds perpetrated against Medicaid.

Books

M. Mendelson, *Tender Loving Greed* (New York: Knopf, 1974). *This book is considered one of the best on the nursing home problem. It examines extensively the corruption that has plagued the industry.* Mendelson has visited over 200 homes throughout the country. Senator Charles Percy, *Growing Old in the Country of the Young* (1974). This is a very critical assessment of nursing homes in the U.S.

The New York Times

"Fraud Is Alleged at Nursing Homes," Nov. 15, 1974, p. 38; "Alternatives Seen to Nursing Homes For Aged Infirm," Oct. 10, 1974, p. 42;
"Nursing Homes Here Linked by Interlocking Leadership," Oct. 9, 1974, p. 85;
"Nursing Homes Use a Variety of Fiscal Ruses to Lift Profits Above 10% Allowed by Law," Oct. 8, 1974, p. 1.
(All page citations are from city editions.)

State Reports

Massachusetts Nursing Home Ombudsman Project, *6th Quarterly Report*, 19 (1974);
Michigan Nursing Home Ombudsman Project Report (June 1973-Nov. 1974);
Pennsylvania Nursing Home Ombudsman Project Final Report, 4-5 (July 1, 1972-June 30, 1974).

5. Differences That Count

The medical standards are imposed on nursing homes. Ontario regulation 196/72 (s. 46[1]) provides that a resident, next of kin, or where they are unavailable, the administrator shall retain a physician to attend residents and provide them with medical care.

Subsection (3) of section 46 requires the physician to review the resident's diet and medication every three months; to do a physical examination of the resident annually (or bi-annually in the case of residents receiving extended care) and to make such additional attendances as the residents' condition requires. Section 47 provides the administrator with a mechanism for replacing a physician who fails to meet these requirements.

Similarly, under the heading of Nursing Care, Section 51 requires that every resident shall be given nursing care in accordance with his needs. Those needs are to be the subject of reassessment on a regular basis. The nursing staff is required to devise a care plan for each resident on the basis of the assessments of such needs.

Records

s. 84. The administrator of a nursing home shall
(a) maintain a separate personal file for each resident; and
(b) maintain in each resident's file
(i) the medical and drug record of the resident, and
(ii) a written record of all other matters that are relevant to the resident;

s. 85. The medical record of a resident shall include
(i) the resident's medical history;
(ii) the written report of each physical examination of the resident by a physician;
(iii) diagnoses;
(iv) orders for treatment of the resident including
(a) orders for the administration of drugs,
(b) orders for medication,
(c) follow-up notes indicating the resident's condition at each visit, signed by the physician attending the resident (O. Reg. 508/72),
(d) a written copy of every telephone order for treatment of the resident given by a physician,
(e) where the resident is an extended care resident, daily nursing notes that record every significant change in the resident's condition signed by the nurse in charge of the resident.

Accidents

s. 91(5). Every occurrence in a nursing home of fire, assault, injury, communicable disease or death resulting from accident or an undetermined cause shall be reported forthwith in full detail . . . to the Director of Nursing Homes.

The regulations governing government-run homes for the aged establish a quite different standard for medical care.

Medical Services

18.(1) In this section, and in section 19 "attending physician" means a legally qualified medical practitioner other than the physician for a home who is appointed under subsection 4 of section 11 of the Act. Ontario Reg. 325/61, s. 6; Ontario Reg. 219/67, s. 8.

(2) All medical and paramedical services, programmes, procedures and medications provided or used in a home are subject to the approval of the physician for the home (O. Reg. 221/69, s. 11[1]).

(3) At least once a year, or at such other more frequent intervals as the board of committee of management of a home requires, the physician for the home shall submit to the board or committee, as the case may be, a report summarizing the general health conditions of the residents and the medical and nursing services provided to them and shall include in the report any recommendations that he considers necessary to ensure proper conditions of health and an adequate state of well-being for all residents (O. Reg. 325/61, s. 6; amended).

(4) The physician for the home shall
(a) inspect the sanitary conditions in the home at least once a month;
(b) report on such inspections to the board or committee of management of the home; and
(c) take any steps that he considers necessary to ensure that any of his recommendations for the correction of any insanitary condition is carried out (Ontario Reg. 325/61, s. 6/O. Reg. 221/69, s. 11(2), amended).

(5) Before admission to a home an applicant shall be given a chest X-ray and the results shall be negative for tuberculosis (Ontario Reg. 219/67, s.9).

(6) A least once a year each resident of a home shall be given a chest X-ray unless otherwise directed by the physician for the home (Ontario Reg. 219/67, s.9).
(7) At the time of his admission to a home and thereafter at least once a year each resident shall be given a medical examination by the physician for the home or the attending physician (Ontario Reg. 219/67, s.9).

(8) Within seven days of the resident's admission thereto, the physician for the home or the attending physician shall make a detailed written report in Form 5 of the results, including any recommendation pertaining thereto, of the medical examination of the resident made at the time of admission, and thereafter shall make a written report of each subsequent medical examination in Form 5 and the report shall be kept with the other records of the resident (Ontario Reg. 219/67, s. 9).

(9) Where the physician for the home or the attending physician directs, a resident of a home shall be given a special diet (Ontario Reg. 219/67, s. 9).

19. The physician for the home shall attend and prescribe medication or medical care for any resident of the home who has no attending physician of his own or who requests that the services of the physician for the home be made available (Ontario Reg. 219/67, s.10).

NOTES: Chapter Eight

1. Words From a Country Doctor

The story of Doctor David Lander is not told in books. It is a matter which has surfaced in the press. See, for example, E. Reid, "About Churches," *The Albertan*, June 20, 1975, and E. Smith, "Elderly Overdrugged and Denied Privacy, Doctor Charges," *The Calgary Herald*, February 24, 1977, p. 45. Before "retiring" to a geriatric practice Doctor Lander spent considerable time treating alcoholics. He found an enormous capacity for self-cure on the part of patients. The doctor's tools go far beyond drugs and surgery. He said: "The only doctor who doesn't have to practice psychotherapy is the pathologist."

Old age, death and society's reaction to them are dealt with by Simone de Beauvoir in *The Coming of Age* (New York: Warner Paperback ed., 1973, translated by P. O'Brien.) She writes (pp. 450-51):

> For those who do not choose to go under, being old means fighting against age. That is the harsh new aspect of their condition: living can no longer be taken for granted. At forty, a healthy man is biologically free to do what he likes. He can push himself to the utmost limits of his strength — he knows he will soon regain it. The danger of sickness or accident does not frighten him overmuch — except in extremely serious cases he will get well and return to his former state. The aged man is obliged to take care of himself: excessive effort might cause heart-failure; an illness would leave him permanently weakened; he would never, or only very slowly, recover from an accident, since his wounds take a long time to heal. Fighting is forbidden to him: he is sure to get the worst of it and he would only make himself ridiculous by starting any violence. He can no longer run fast enough to take part in any political manifestations, and he would be a burden to his younger companions. Mental and physical work, exercise and even amusements tire him. The elderly man often suffers from exactly located or generalized pains that take away all his pleasure in life. Colette was tortured by her rheumatism. An admirer congratulated her upon her fame and her apparent happiness; she replied, "Yes, my dear, but age is there". "But apart from age?" "Still more age."

2. Being Free

The story of the Trotscha family is told by B. Yaffe, "Man Dies in Own Home, Widow Finds It a Costly Comfort," *The Globe and Mail*, May 17, 1977, p. 5. Mrs. Trotscha added: "I have no money for a monument for my husband, but in his memory I am going to fight so other people won't have to go through what I had to go through. This is wrong, totally wrong." Peter Trotscha, the couple's 27-year-old son, said, "We had to use up a lot of our personal strength to fight the system of home health care. Believe me, you have to really fight for these services. My father is dead, but we're concerned now with those people who don't have the energy to fight." He said he had received a number of "abusive" phone calls from a home care coordinator who "put pressure on me to give support to my parents to pay for the hospital bed. She also said it would be best to get him into a nursing home or chronic-care hospital."

Emily Meyer, the home care coordinator who dealt with the Trotschas, said, "We have to investigate all the alternatives (once the home care services are cut off) and she [Mrs. Trotscha] became upset with some of the suggestions. She was a very upset woman." The 54-year-old Mrs. Trotscha said she didn't want "to go begging for money to relatives and friends. We wanted to keep our independence."

In 1974 the *Ontario Task Force on Long Term Care* made these recommendations which have yet to be fully implemented:

1. The Ministry broaden its policies determining eligibility criteria for admission to Home Care to provide for long-term care patients, and

2. Make provision in the Home Care Programme for a preventive level of care.

3. All institutional admission stations adopt, as a routine, the determination of whether or not the health needs of the applicant for admission to the institution can be adequately met in the Home Care Programme before admission to the institution.

4. The Ministry, together with the Ministry of Community & Social Services, work toward elimination of the apparent overlap and confusion that exists between the programmes provided by the Ministry of Health in Home Care, and by the Ministry of Community & Social Services under the Homemaker & Nurses Services Act.

Communal, or congregate living for the elderly exists in both Canada and the United States, although government gives it less than full support. Judith Wax provides an in-depth view of one commune, The Weinfeld Group, a total of 12 persons, in Evanston, Illinois, in "Pooling the Strengths of Age in a New Kind of Commune," *The New York Times Magazine*, November 21, 1976. Most of the 12 communal members had lived alone, or with relatives, in nursing homes, or even psychiatric hospitals before moving to Weinfeld. Ms. Wax writes (pp. 38, 40):

> Like similar innovations in Philadelphia and Bethesda, Md., Weinfeld depends on funding and strong backup social services from an outside agency. Adapted from programs studied in England and Sweden, Weinfeld is one of many projects supported by the Council for Jewish Elderly, an offshoot of the Jewish Federation of Metropolitan Chicago. The aim is to encourage each resident's independence by maintaining community and family ties while providing only as much help — counselling, homemaking, health care — as is needed, no more, no less. That demands careful staffing: a cook and "careworker" on site daily, a part-time activities therapist, a domestic who comes twice a week, a nurse who comes when she is needed and a nutritionist who visits to plan menus and special diets. "Our baby sitter," a college student, sleeps in each night; council social workers are on call, and a psychiatrist helps screen candidates for the traits that will make them compatible members of the Weinfeld group.
>
> It costs $500 a month to live at Weinfeld, and few of the residents can swing the full amount, even with Social Security benefits and some family supplements. Jewish Federation philanthropy makes up the difference. "Weinfeld costs half what would be spent by the taxpayers if these same people were institutionalized," says Ronald Weismehl, the council's executive director. "But when government is unable to meet needs, sectarian agencies have to do it as innovators."
>
> The U-shaped complex of town-houses, located on a quiet, middle class street and convenient to shopping, cultural and religious centers, makes an ideal setting for the experiment. After its purchase in 1971, the one-story complex was remodeled into one big home; dividing walls were torn down so that residents can stroll to each other's living rooms and the communal dining and recreation rooms at the center. You can't be a recluse at Weinfeld, but privacy is easy; each of the six units, shared by two residents, has two bedrooms, a bathroom, a spacious living room and a door to the outside that may be used

at will. Nobody needs to ask permission to be part of the world. Most prized: the small private kitchens, for snacks, treats and breakfast at any hour one chooses. Colours and fabrics are different in each unit, and though the basics are provided, residents are encouraged to add on — plants, photographs, old treasures and new handicrafts. Hung over the entrance to one woman's bedroom, a cherished stole keeps perpetual vigil; long retired from active duty, it is permanent decor.

The role of medicine in personal health is developed by Ivan Illich in *Limits to Medicine–Medical Nemesis: The Expropriation of Health* (Toronto: McClelland & Stewart, 1976.) See pp. 274-75. Somewhat related to the Illich critique is that set out by Elisabeth Kubler-Ross in *Death and Dying* (New York: paperback ed.; Macmillan Publishing Co., 1969), p. 17:

> Though every man will attempt in his own way to postpone such questions and issues until he is forced to face them, he will only be able to change things if he can start to conceive of his own death. This cannot be done on a mass level. This cannot be done by computers. This has to be done by every human being alone. Each one of us has the need to avoid this issue, yet each one of us has to face it sooner or later. If all of us could make a start by contemplating the possibility of our own personal death, we may effect many things, most important of all the welfare of our patients, our families, and finally perhaps our nation.

Bibliography

Books

Baum, D. *The Final Plateau: The Betrayal of Our Older Citizens.* Toronto: Burns and MacEachern, 1974.

Canadian Conference on Social Welfare. *Extended Care Facilities for the Chronically Ill.* Ottawa: Canadian Welfare Council, 1969.

De Beauvoir, S. *The Coming of Age.* Translated by P. O'Brien. New York: Warner paperback, 1973.

Illich, I. *Limits to Medicine – Medical Nemesis: The Expropriation of Health.* Toronto: McClelland and Stewart, 1976.

Kubler-Ross, E. *Death and Dying.* New York: Macmillian Publishing Co., 1969.

Nursing Department Manual. Ontario Ministry of Health, 1974.

Posner, J. *"Perceptions of Physical and Mental Incompetence in a Home for the Aged."* Doctoral thesis. Toronto, York University, 1975.

Proceedings of the Institute on Long Term Care. Co-Sponsored by The Ontario Hospital Association, Ontario Association of Homes for the Aged, Ontario Nursing Home Association, Dec. 2-3, 1974. Toronto: Ontario Homes for the Aged Centre.

Residential and Community Services for Old People. Canada Council on Social Development, 1975.

Role of the Adjuvant in Ontario's Home for the Aged. Ontario Senior Citizens Bureau, 1974.

The Role of the Inquest in Today's Litigation. Toronto: Law Society of Upper Canada, 1975.

Shulman, M. *Coroner.* Markham: Simon and Schuster Ltd., 1975.

Special Senate Committee on Aging. Ottawa: Queen's Printer, 1966.

Townsend, C. *Old Age: The Last Segregation,* (Nader Report). New York: Grossman Publishers (Bantam ed.), 1971.

Twentieth Canadian Conference on Social Welfare. Vancouver: 1966; *Programs For the Aged.* Ottawa: Canadian Welfare Council, 1968.

Reports

Alberta Inquiry into the Alleged Excessive Use of Force at the Calgary Correctional Institute. Edmonton: 1973.

Annual Report of the Ontario Advisory Council on Senior Citizens.

Barstow, D. "Demographic and Economic Aspects of Housing Canada's Elderly," Central Mortgage and Housing Corporation Policy Planning Division. Ottawa: 1973.

Building Better, A Survey of Ontario Homes for the Aged as Viewed by Residents and by an Independent Group of Senior Citizens. Associated Senior Executives of Canada Limited. Toronto: 1974.

Consider Yourself at Home. Toronto Department of Social and Family Services, 1971.

Housing Our Elderly. Central Mortgage and Housing Corporation. Revised Edition. Ottawa.

"Implications of the Changing Age Structure of the Canadian Population," *Study on Population and Technology Perceptions*, 2. Ottawa: Science Council of Canada, 1976.

Inquiry into Certain Disturbances at Kingston Prison during 1971. Ottawa: Information Canada, 1973.

Mayor's Task Force Report on the Disabled and Elderly. Toronto: 1974.

Ontario Task Force on Long Term Care. Toronto: Queen's Printer, 1974.

"Population, Technology, and Resources," Report No. 25. Ottawa: Science Council of Canada, 1976.

Report of the Ontario Council of Health, Senior Advisory Body to the Minister of Health: A Review of the Ontario Health Insurance Plan. Ontario Council of Health. Toronto: 1973.

Report of the Ontario Interministerial Committee on Residential Services to the Cabinet Committee on Social Development. Toronto: Queen's Printer, 1975.

"Poverty in Canada," *Report of the Special Senate Committee*. Ottawa: Queen's Printer, 1971.

Report to the Solicitor General's Working Group On Federal Maximum Security Designs. Ottawa Information Canada, 1971.

Social Planning Council of Metropolitan Toronto Study Committee on Homes for the Aged. Toronto: 1963.

Summary of the First Ontario Residents Council Conference. Toronto: Ministry of Community and Social Services, 1973.

This Is My Life and This Is My Home, Survey of Regional Municipality of Niagara Homes for Senior Citizens. Residents Council of the Niagara Region Homes for Senior Citizens, 1974.

Transcript Summation of Doctor Margaret Milton In the Coroner's Court, Municipality of Metropolitan Toronto, Inquest into the Death of Bertha Richardson, 1976.

"Questions of the Elderly and the Aged," *United Nations Report of the Secretary-General*. New York: 1973.

Articles

Aldrich C. and Mendoff, E. "Relocation of the Aged and Disabled: A Mortality Study," 11, *Journal of the American Geriatrics Society*, 1963, 185.

Clark, D. "As a Matter of Caring," *Canadian Welfare*, July-August, 1974, 16.

"Don't Put Me In A Home — Woman 85," *The Toronto Star*, February 19, 1977, A12.

Downes, G. "Must a Transfer Order be a Death Sentence for S.N.F. Patients?" *Modern Health Care*, October 1974, 44.

Garrison, D. "Alberta, The Best Province to Grow Old In," *Chatelaine*, February 1973, 84.

Grauer H. and Birnbom, F. "A Geriatric Functional Rating Scale to Determine the Need for Institutional Care," *Journal of the American Geriatrics Society*, 23, 1975, 472.

Killian, E. "Effects of Geriatrics Transfers on Mortality Rates," *Social Work*, January 1970, 19.

Markus, N. "Home Care for the Aged" *On Growing Old*, 12, 1973, 1.

Ogren E. and Linn, M. "Male Nursing Home Patients: Relocation and Mortality," *Journal of the American Geriatrics Society*, 19, 1971, 229.

Prock, V. "Effects of Institutionalization: A Comparison of Community, Waiting List, and Institutionalized Aged Persons," *American Journal of Public Health*, 59, 1969, 1837.

Schwenger, C. W. "Keeping Old Folks at Home," *Canadian Journal of Public Health*, 65, 1974, 417.

Skerman, R. "Bringing the Quality of Life to Nursing Home Residents," *Hospital Administration in Canada*, July 1976, 30.

Van Rijn, N. "Care Inadequate at Nursing Homes Jury Says," *The Toronto Star*, March 5, 1977, A2.

Wax, J. "Pooling the Strengths of Age in a New Kind of Commune," *The New York Times Magazine*, Nov. 2, 1976, 23.

Legislation

ALBERTA

Health Care Insurance Act, Statutes of Alberta 1969, Chapter 90, and Regulations.

Nursing Home Act, Revised Statutes of Alberta 1970, Chapter C. 264 and Regulations.

Senior Citizens Housing Act, Statutes of Alberta, 1973, Chapter 54 and Regulations.

BRITISH COLUMBIA

The Hospital Insurance Act, Revised Statutes of British Columbia, 1960, Chapter 180 and Regulations.

MANITOBA

The Hospital Services Insurance Act, Revised Statutes of Manitoba, 1970, Chapter H-140 and Regulations.

NEW BRUNSWICK

Medical Services Payment Act, Revised Statutes of New Brunswick, 1968.

NEWFOUNDLAND

Hospital Agreement Act, Statutes of Newfoundland, 1957, Chapter 60, and Regulations.

NOVA SCOTIA

The Hospital Insurance Act, Revised Statutes of Nova Scotia, 1967, Chapter 125, and Regulations.

ONTARIO

Health Service Insurance Act, Revised Statutes of Ontario, Chapter 200, and Regulations.

Home for the Aged and Rest Home Act, Revised Statutes of Ontario, Chapter 206, and Regulations.

The Civil Rights Statute Law Amendment Act, Statutes of Ontario, 1971, Chapter 50, Section 46.

An Act to Amend the Home for the Aged and Rest Home Act, Statutes of Ontario, 1972, Chapter 62.

An Act to Amend the Home for the Aged and Rest Home Act, Statutes of Ontario, 1972, Chapter 148.

An Act to Amend the Home for the Aged and Rest Home Act, Statutes of Ontario, 1972, Chapter 27.

The Nursing Home Act, Statutes of Ontario, 1972, Chapter 11, and Regulations.

An Act to Amend the Nursing Home Act, Statutes of Ontario, 1973, Chapter 38.

PRINCE EDWARD ISLAND

The Hospital and Diagnostic Services Insurance Act, Statutes of Prince Edward Island, 1959, Chapter 17, and Regulations.

QUEBEC

Hospital Insurance Act, Statutes of Quebec, 1970, Volume 4, Chapter 163, and Regulations.

Health Services and Social Services Act, Statutes of Quebec, 1971, Chapter 48, Article 149.

SASKATCHEWAN

Housing and Special Care Homes Act, Revised Statutes of Saskatchewan, 1965, Chapter 275, and Regulations.

The Saskatchewan Medical Care Act, Revised Statutes of Saskatchewan, 1965, Chapter 255, and Regulations.

INDEX

A

Adjuvants   50-52
Alberta   78, 108-110

B

Baycrest Centre For Geriatric Care   19, 20, 32, 35, n.132
British Columbia   77-78, 112-113

C

Coroner, role of   98-100
    Medical care, quality reviewed   98-108
    Nature of investigations   98-102
    Milton, Margaret   99, 101-102, 107
    Shulman, Morton   99-100
    Recommendations of coroner's jury   105-106
Canada
    Statistics on age   3, 4, 26, n.125
    Housing   5, 6
    Statistics on daycare   9, 10
    Employment statistics   11, 12
    Government expenditure   23
    Old Age Security   82
    Guaranteed Income Supplement   82-84
    Canada Pension Plan   83
      Comparison of Insurance Plans   n.164-167
    Senate Study on Aging   5, 9-12
    Central Mortgage Housing Corporation   5, 16-19, 21

E

Employment Statistics (see Canada)
Extendicare Ltd.   22
    — Subsidies   35
    — Standards   61-65
    — Financial costs   74-79
    — Changing policy   79-82

G

Great Britain
    Statistics on daycare   8, 9
    Basic needs   n.127-128
Grievance procedure, institutions for the aged   67-68
Guaranteed Income Supplement (see Canada)

H

Home Care   5-12
Hospitals, relationship between institutions for the aged   72-76
Housing
    Goals and results   13-16
    Privacy   23, 25, 25

I

Illich, Ivan   116

L

Law
— Quebec experience   57-60, n.149-150
— Ontario experience   60-65, n.150-152
— Inspection   65-71
Lander, Dr. David   100-110, n.178

M

Montreal, Maimonides Home for the Aged   43-46

N

Newfoundland   77
Nova Scotia   78
Nursing Homes
    Standards for admission   27, n.135-136
      — case study   27-31
    Procedures for admission   31, 38, 39, n.136-141
    Life in the home   40-46, 110-112, n.145-148
      — residents councils   44-49
      — food   48-50
    Employees   n.152-153
    — adjuvants   51, 52
    — inspectors   65-71, n.156-157
    Environment   53-56
    and the law   57, n.154-156
    Financial costs   72-82, 112, 113, n.160-163
    Physicians standards   100-107
    Bureaucracy
      — case study   113-115, n.179
      — In Canada   n.123-125
      — Statistics   n.158, 159

O

Old Age Security (see Canada)
Ombudsman   81-82
Ontario
    Statistics on age   4, 5
    Statistics on homes   10
    Central Mortgage and Housing Corporation   16, 21,
        n.131-132
    Nursing home closings   35
    Ontario Hospital Association   37
    Inspection regulations   65-71
    Financial costs/nursing homes   72-79
    Guaranteed Annual Income System   81, 83-86, n.129-131,
        n.164-167
    Coroner
    — inquiry, inquest, standards   98-107, n.168-171
    Physicians Standards   100-107, n.175-177

P

Pensioners Concerned   119
Prisons, analogy to institutions for the aged   46-48
Privacy, right to   23

Q

Quebec experience,   57-60
    Regulation of nursing homes, eliminating profit   58
    Underground nursing homes   59-60

S

Saskatchewan, inspection of nursing homes   66
Scapegoating   45-46

T

Toronto, Mayor's Task Force on Housing   15-16

U

United Nations, Survey of Aging Populations   3-4
United States
— Regulations   66-67
Ralph Nader Study   100
— General facts/statistics   n.171-175
— Communal nursing home   n.179-181

V

Volunteers, institutions for the aged   53-55